ADRIFT AND ALONE

TRUE STORIES OF SURVIVAL AT SEA

by Nel Yomtov
illustrated by Pat Kinsella

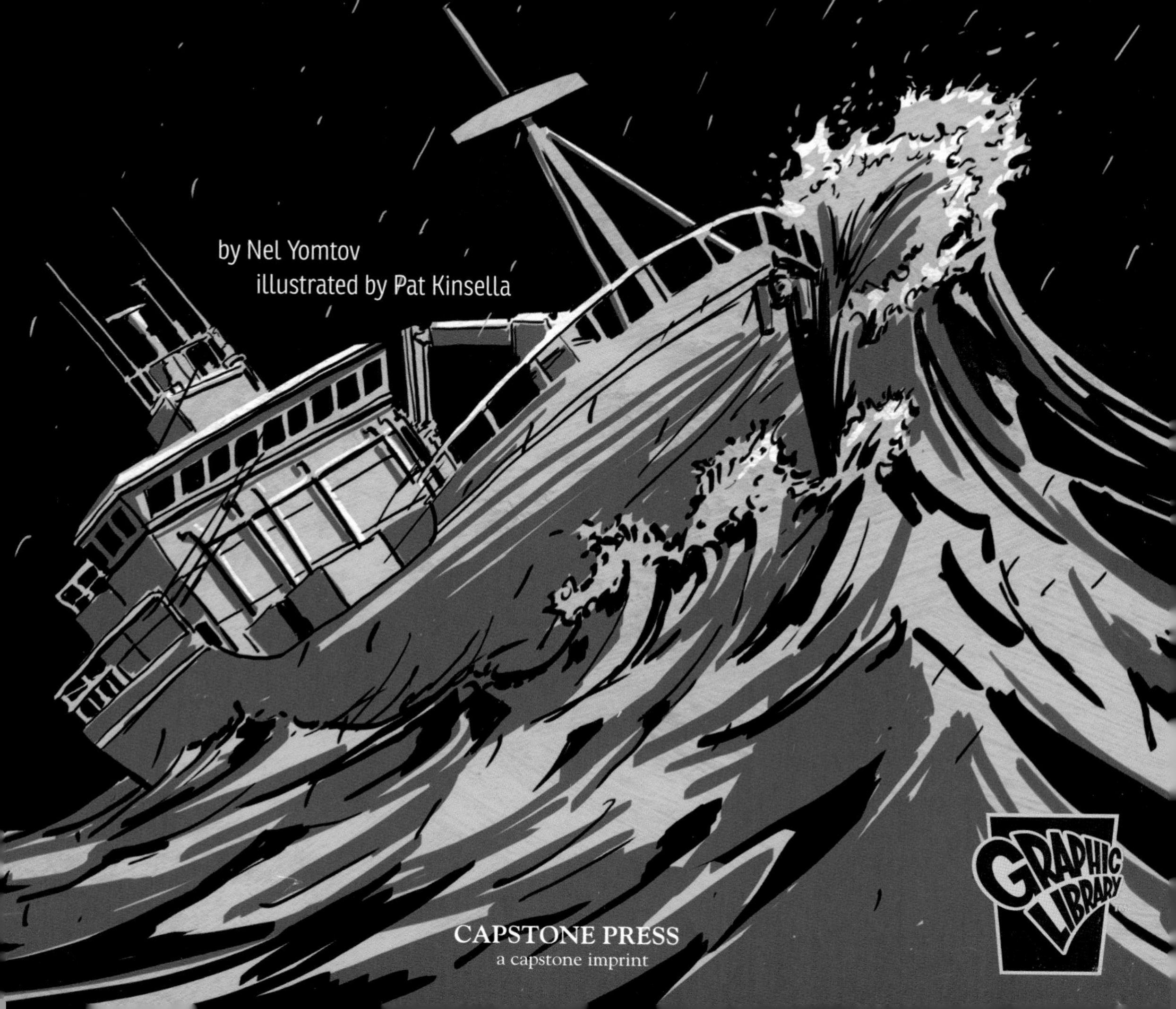

CAPSTONE PRESS
a capstone imprint

Graphic Library is published by Capstone Press,
1710 Roe Crest Drive, North Mankato, Minnesota 56003
www.capstonepub.com

Library of Congress Cataloging-in-Publication Data
Cataloging-in-publication information is on file with the Library
of Congress.
ISBN 978-1-4914-6572-1 (library binding)
ISBN 978-1-4914-6576-9 (eBook PDF)

Editorial Credits:
Anthony Wacholtz, editor; Ashlee Suker, designer; Nathan Gassman,
Creative Director; Laura Manthe, production specialist

Editor's note:
Direct quotations, noted in red type, appear on the following pages:

Page 12, panel 2: Dougal Robertson. Survive the Savage Sea.
    New York: Praeger Publishers, 1973, p. 146.

Page 12, panel 4: Ibid., pp. 194–195.

Page 13: Ibid., p. 207.

Page 16: Steven Callahan. Adrift: Seventy-Six Days Lost at Sea. New
    York: Ballantine, 1996, p. 111.

Page 21: Spike Walker. Nights of Ice. New York: St. Martin's Press,
    1997, p. 83.

Page 23: Richard Phillips. A Captain's Duty. New York: Hyperion,
    2010, p. 151.

Page 24: Ibid., p. 175.

Page 25, panel 1: Ibid., p. 206.

Page 25, panel 5: Ibid., pp. 261–262.

Page 27, both: http://www.gq.com/news-politics/newsmakers/
    201110/hiromitsu-shinkawa-japan-tsunami-rescue-story

Printed in the United States of America
in North Mankato, Minnesota.
102015   009317R

TABLE OF CONTENTS

ALONE AT SEA

Being lost at sea is one of the most challenging survival situations imaginable. Once adrift on vast stretches of endless ocean, a person is at the mercy of nature. Blazing heat, icy waters, powerful storms, huge waves, and dangerous sea creatures such as sharks and whales are constant threats. Castaways can easily die from heatstroke, hunger, or thirst. Hypothermia, a condition in which the body temperature drops dangerously low, can also cause death.

Although surrounded by billions of gallons of water, none of it is safe to drink. Seawater contains salt. Drinking too much saltwater shrinks the cells in the human body. The result can be dehydration, which means the body does not have enough water and fluids to work properly. If left untreated, dehydration can lead to vomiting, hallucinations, and even death.

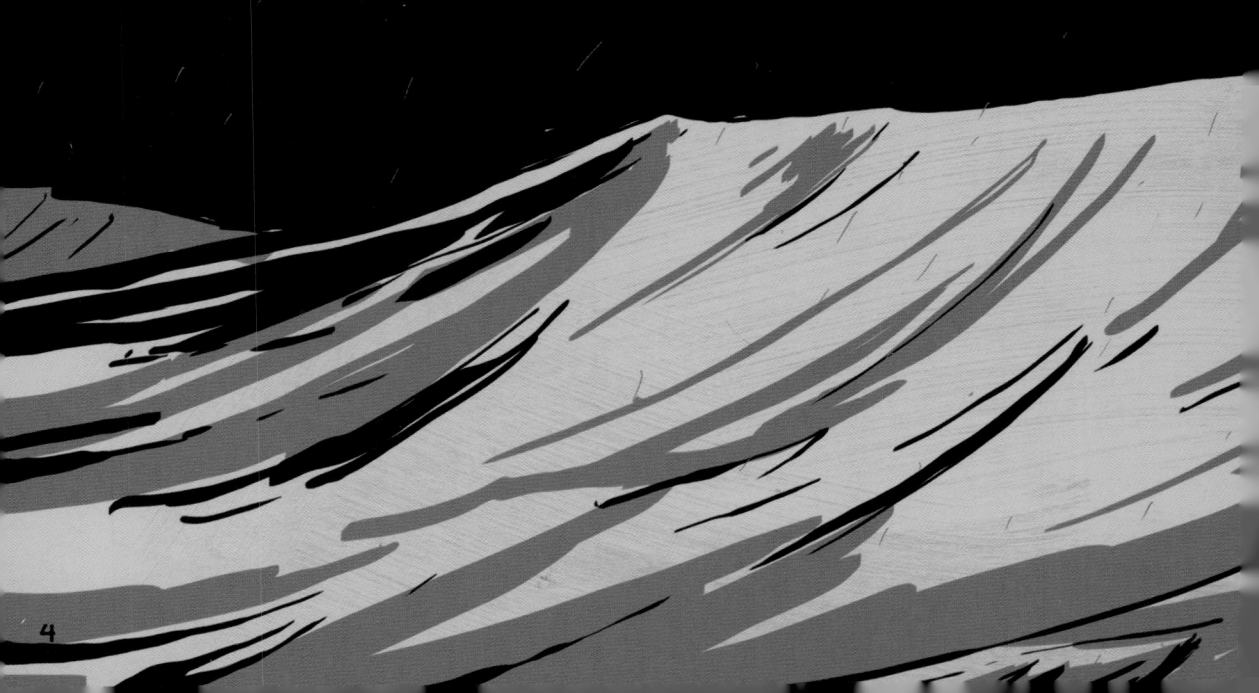

With so many dangers to face, can people truly survive for weeks, or even months, lost at sea? Remarkably, the answer is "Yes!" With courage, patience, and a healthy dose of self-confidence, some amazing castaways have beaten incredible odds. Whether through cleverness, resourcefulness, or just plain stubbornness, the survivors in these true tales didn't panic and never gave up. They conquered death on the high seas and lived to tell their stories.

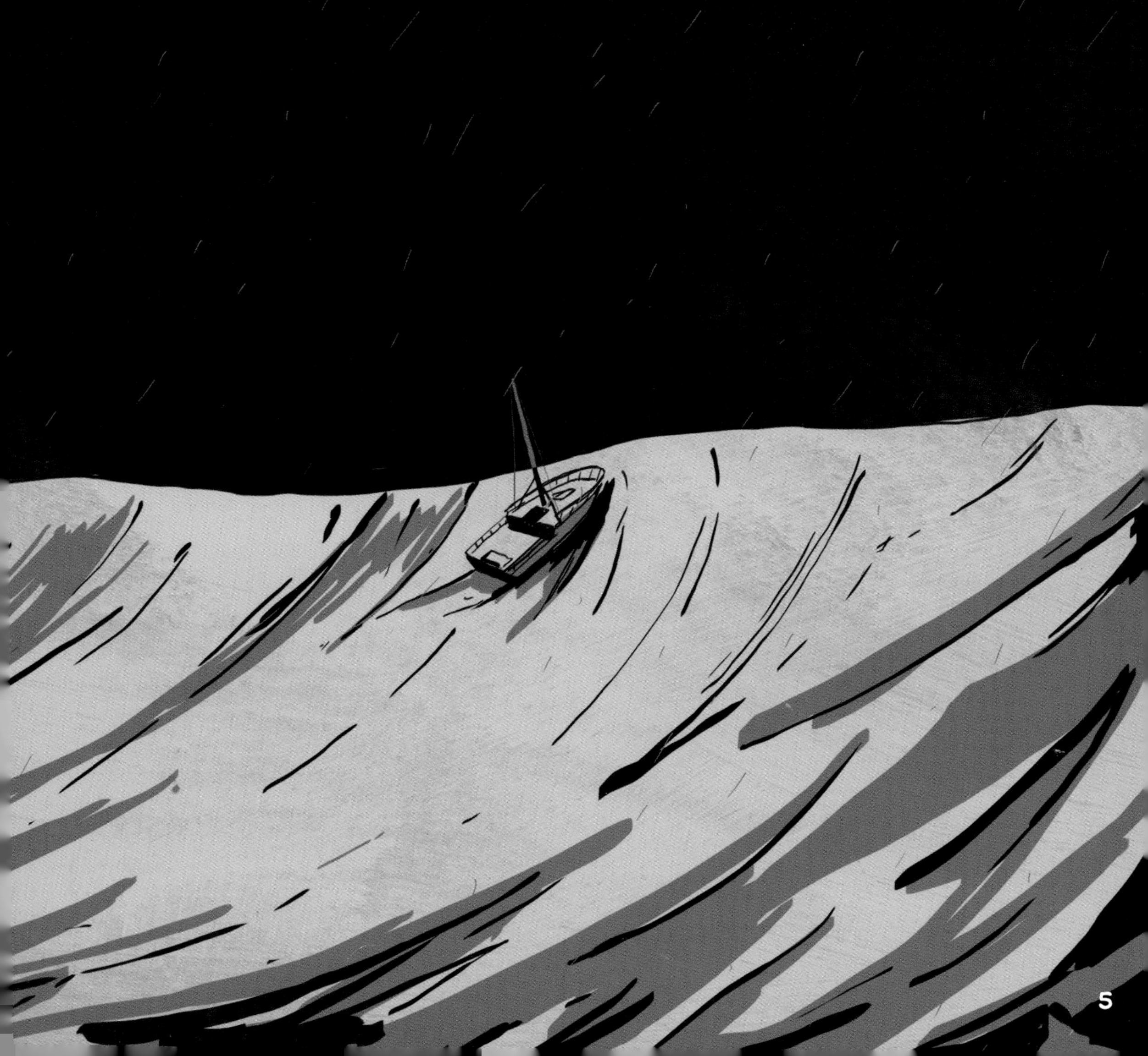

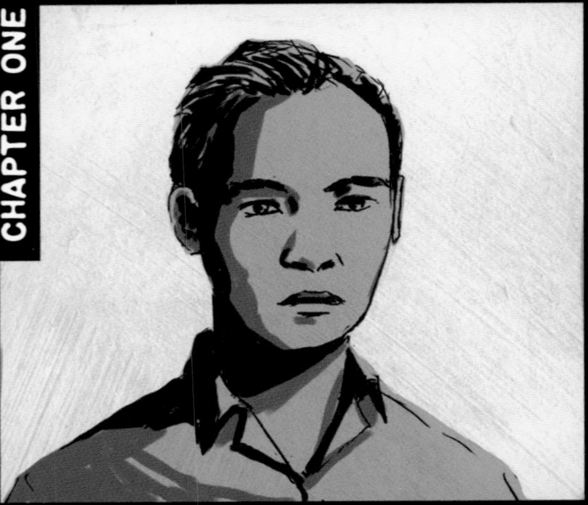

CHAPTER ONE

POON LIM
SOLE SURVIVOR

Poon Lim was a 24-year-old steward working on the British merchant ship SS *Benlomond* during World War II (1939-1945). On November 23, 1942, two torpedoes from a German submarine sunk the ship off the coast of Brazil. Lim grabbed his life jacket and jumped overboard. The other crewmembers of the *Benlomond*—about 55—were lost. Although Poon Lim avoided going down with the ship, he was alone in the ocean.

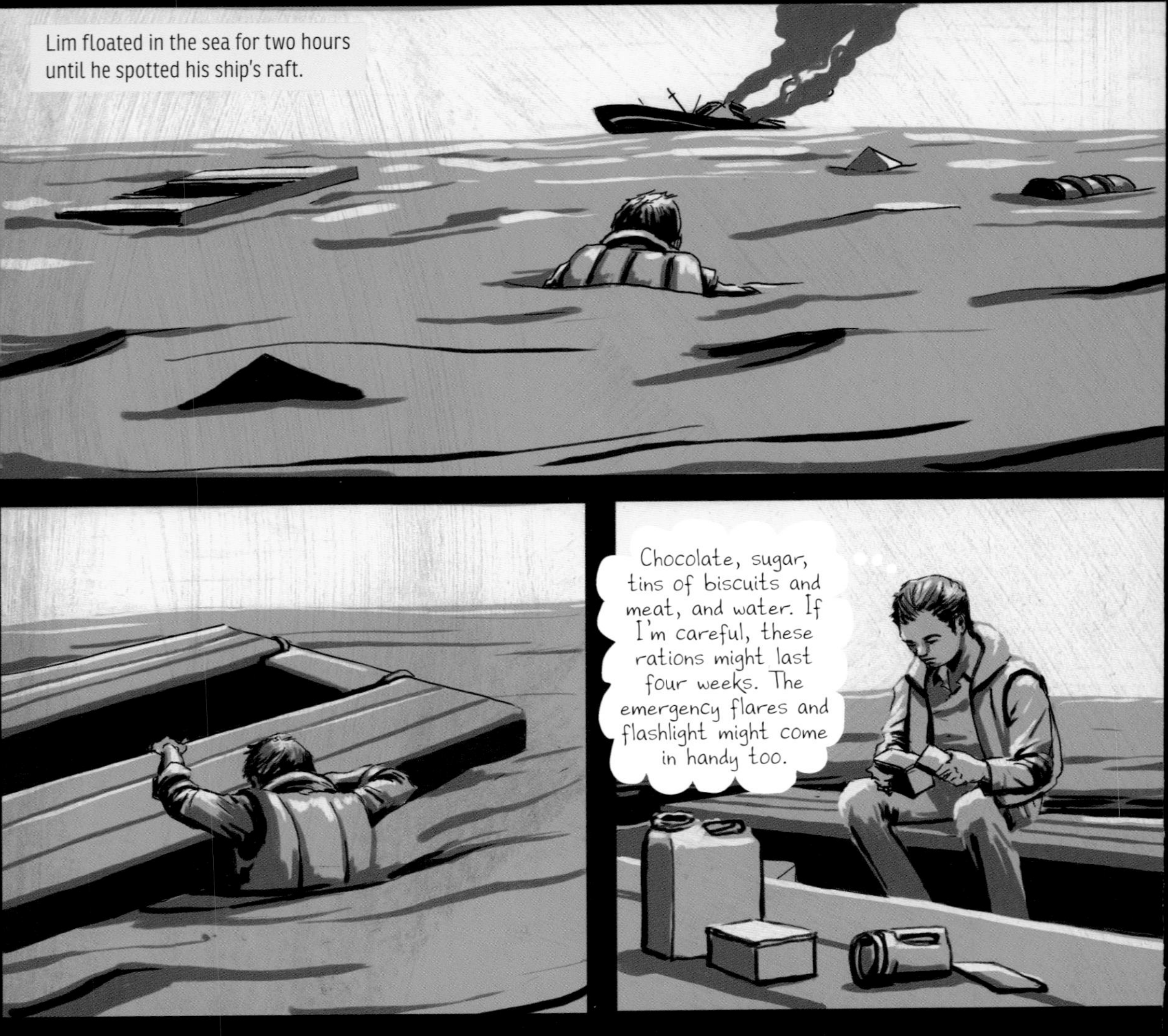
Lim floated in the sea for two hours until he spotted his ship's raft.
Chocolate, sugar, tins of biscuits and meat, and water. If I'm careful, these rations might last four weeks. The emergency flares and flashlight might come in handy too.

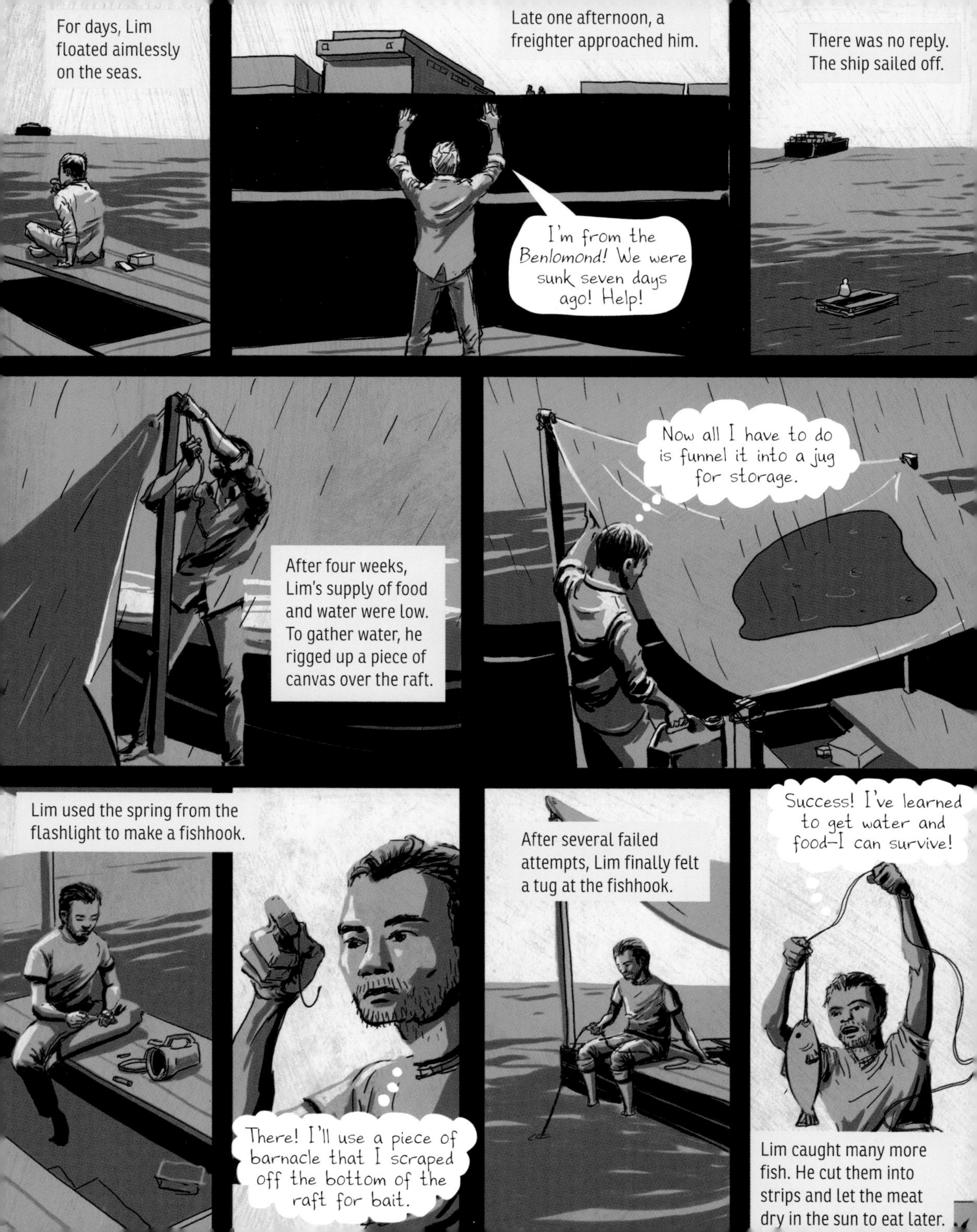
For days, Lim floated aimlessly on the seas.
Late one afternoon, a freighter approached him.
I'm from the Benlomond! We were sunk seven days ago! Help!
There was no reply. The ship sailed off.
After four weeks, Lim's supply of food and water were low. To gather water, he rigged up a piece of canvas over the raft.
Now all I have to do is funnel it into a jug for storage.
Lim used the spring from the flashlight to make a fishhook.
There! I'll use a piece of barnacle that I scraped off the bottom of the raft for bait.
After several failed attempts, Lim finally felt a tug at the fishhook.
Success! I've learned to get water and food—I can survive!
Lim caught many more fish. He cut them into strips and let the meat dry in the sun to eat later.

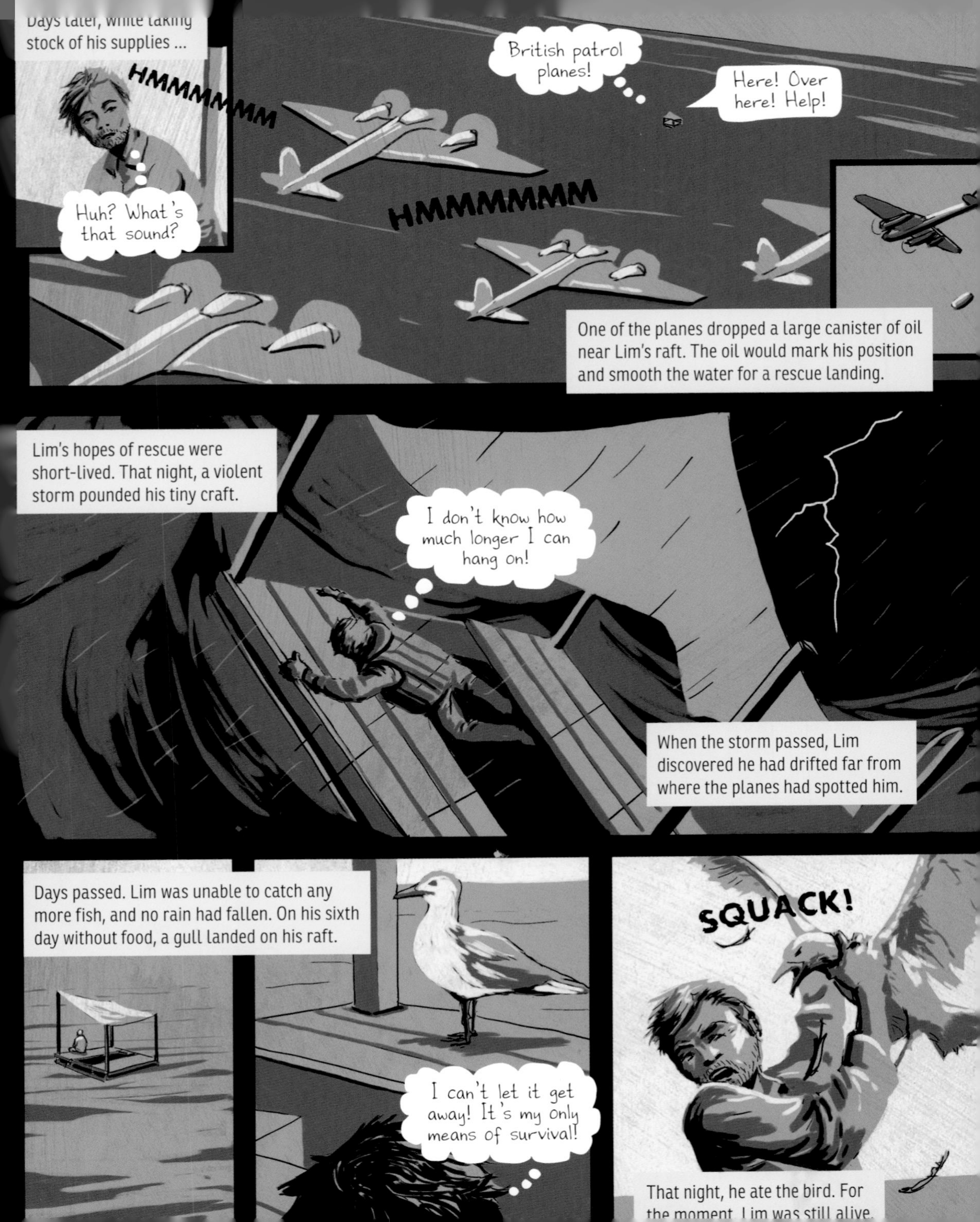
Days later, while taking stock of his supplies ...
HMMMMMMM
Huh? What's that sound?
HMMMMMMM
British patrol planes!
Here! Over here! Help!
One of the planes dropped a large canister of oil near Lim's raft. The oil would mark his position and smooth the water for a rescue landing.
Lim's hopes of rescue were short-lived. That night, a violent storm pounded his tiny craft.
I don't know how much longer I can hang on!
When the storm passed, Lim discovered he had drifted far from where the planes had spotted him.
Days passed. Lim was unable to catch any more fish, and no rain had fallen. On his sixth day without food, a gull landed on his raft.
I can't let it get away! It's my only means of survival!
SQUACK!
That night, he ate the bird. For the moment, Lim was still alive.

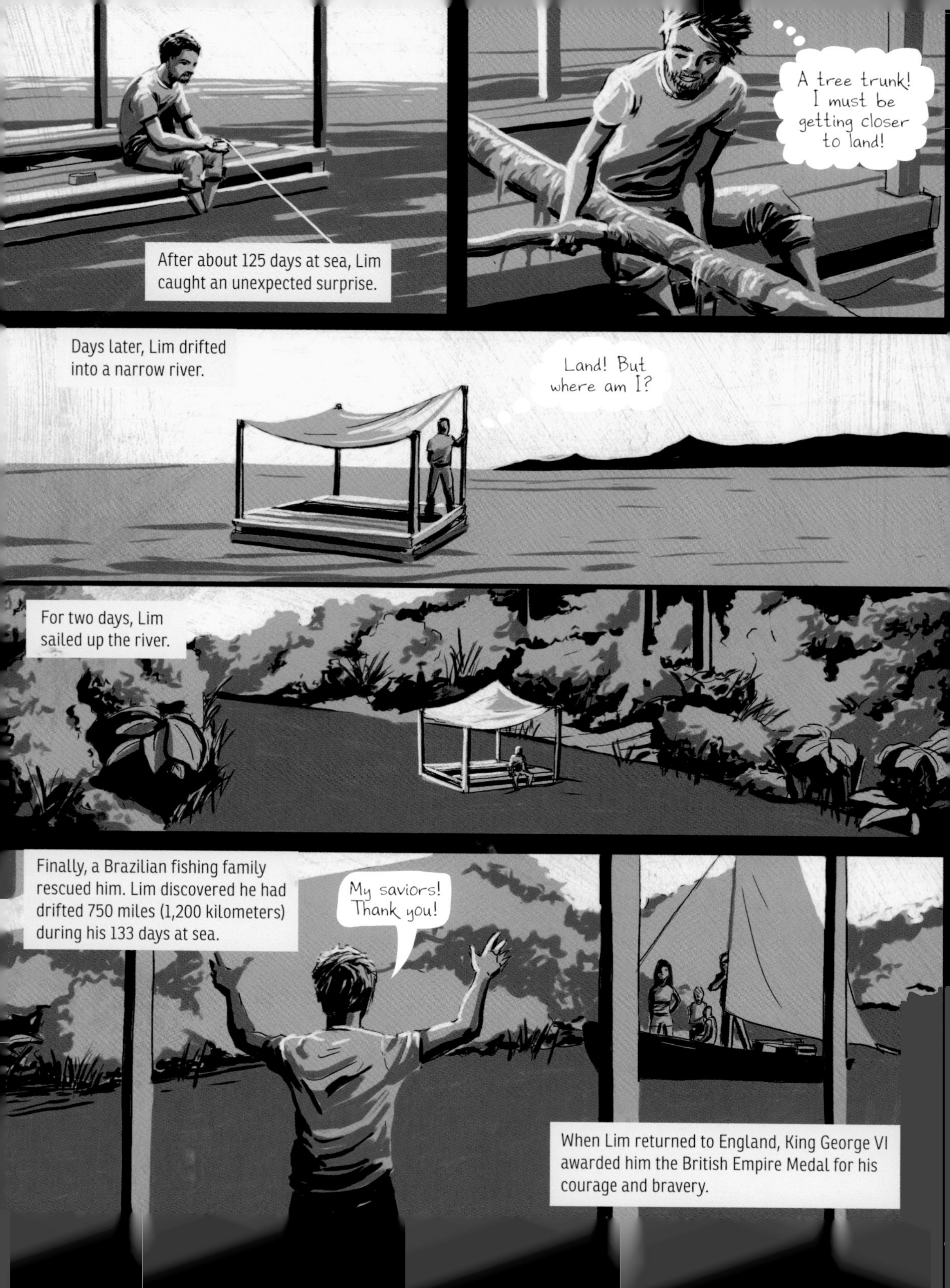
After about 125 days at sea, Lim caught an unexpected surprise.
A tree trunk! I must be getting closer to land!
Days later, Lim drifted into a narrow river.
Land! But where am I?
For two days, Lim sailed up the river.
Finally, a Brazilian fishing family rescued him. Lim discovered he had drifted 750 miles (1,200 kilometers) during his 133 days at sea.
My saviors! Thank you!
When Lim returned to England, King George VI awarded him the British Empire Medal for his courage and bravery.

CHAPTER TWO

THE ROBERTSONS

ATTACKED BY KILLER WHALES

In June 1972 Dougal and Lyn Robertson set sail from Central America. Also on board the *Lucette*, a 43-foot (13-meter) schooner, was their son, Douglas, their twins, Sandy and Neil, and a hitchhiker named Robin Williams. They were bound for the Galapagos Islands.

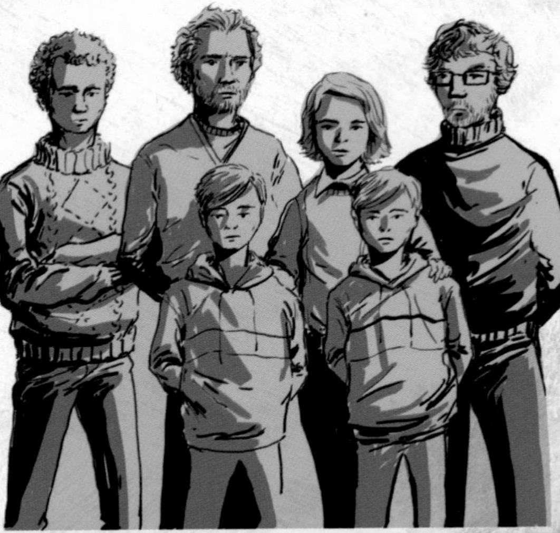

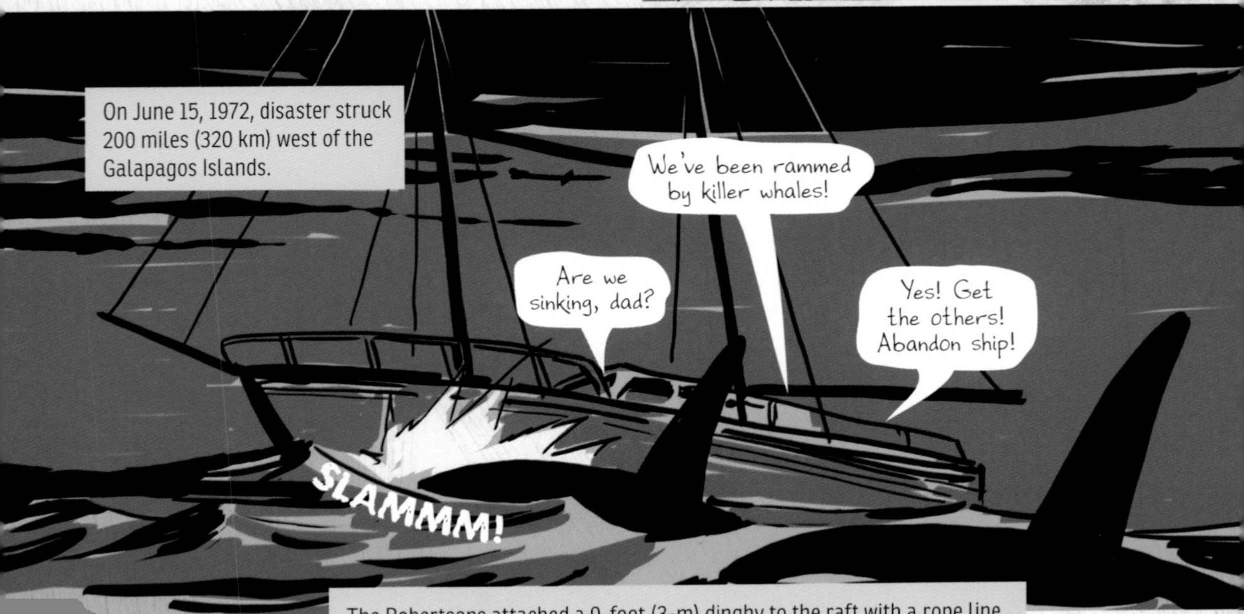
On June 15, 1972, disaster struck 200 miles (320 km) west of the Galapagos Islands.
We've been rammed by killer whales!
Are we sinking, dad?
Yes! Get the others! Abandon ship!
SLAMMMM!

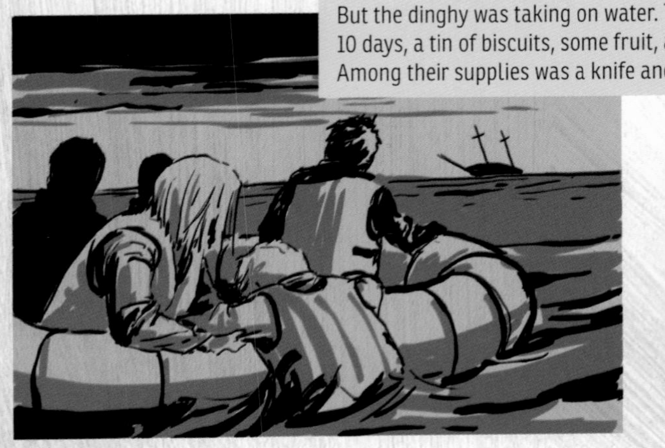
The Robertsons attached a 9-foot (3-m) dinghy to the raft with a rope line. But the dinghy was taking on water. They had only enough fresh water for 10 days, a tin of biscuits, some fruit, and a small amount of other food. Among their supplies was a knife and several emergency flares.

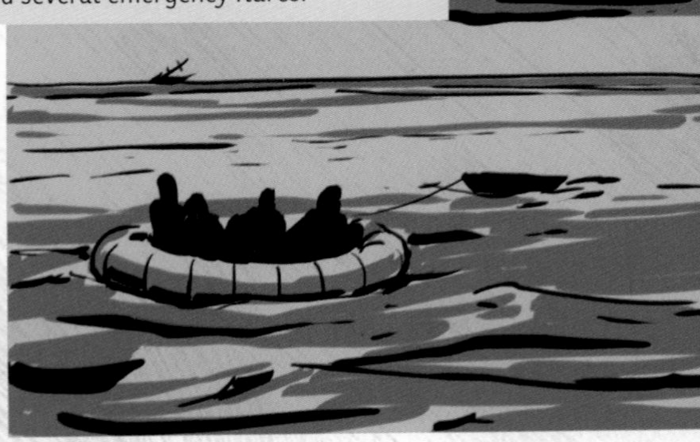

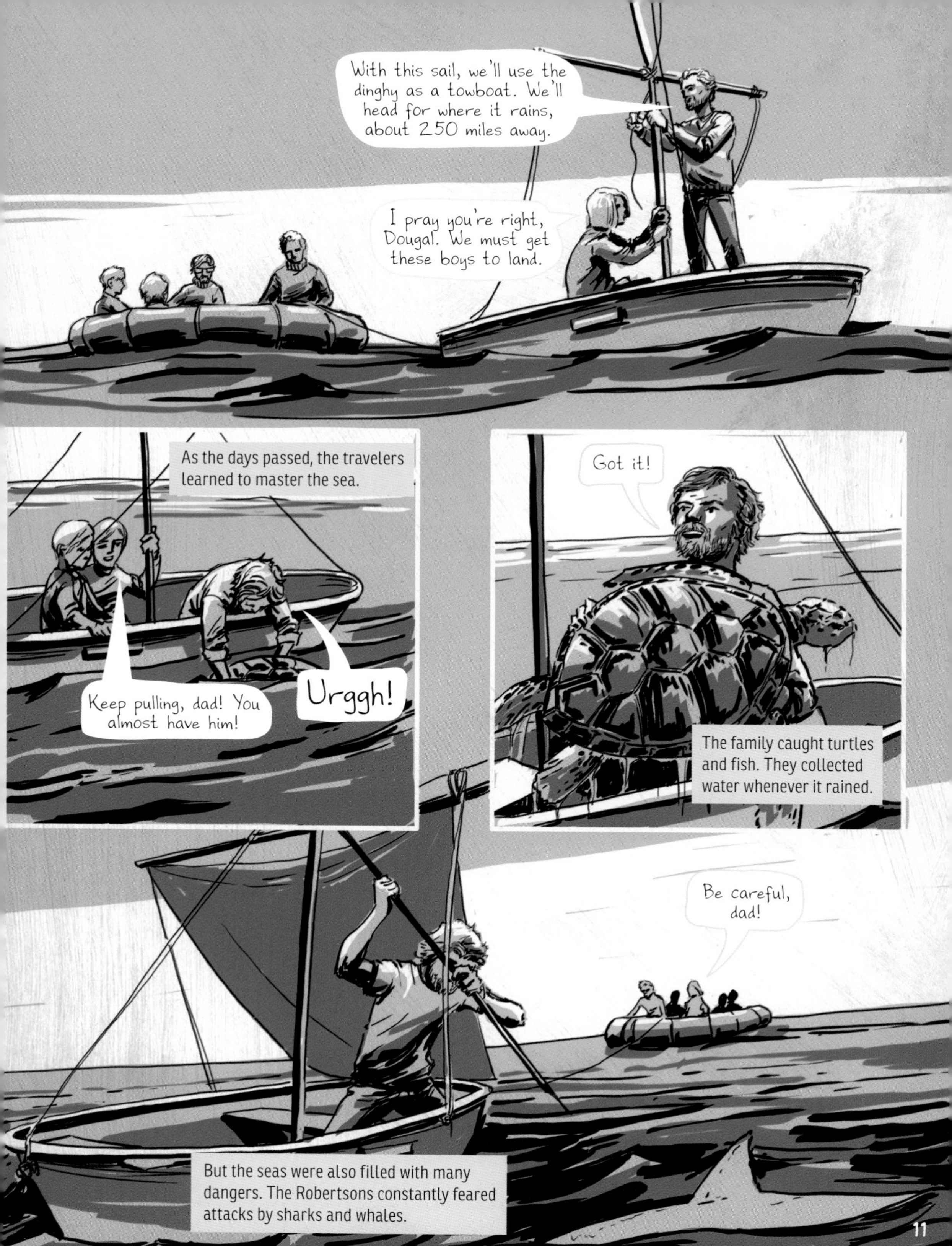
With this sail, we'll use the dinghy as a towboat. We'll head for where it rains, about 250 miles away.
I pray you're right, Dougal. We must get these boys to land.
As the days passed, the travelers learned to master the sea.
Keep pulling, dad! You almost have him!
Urggh!
Got it!
The family caught turtles and fish. They collected water whenever it rained.
Be careful, dad!
But the seas were also filled with many dangers. The Robertsons constantly feared attacks by sharks and whales.

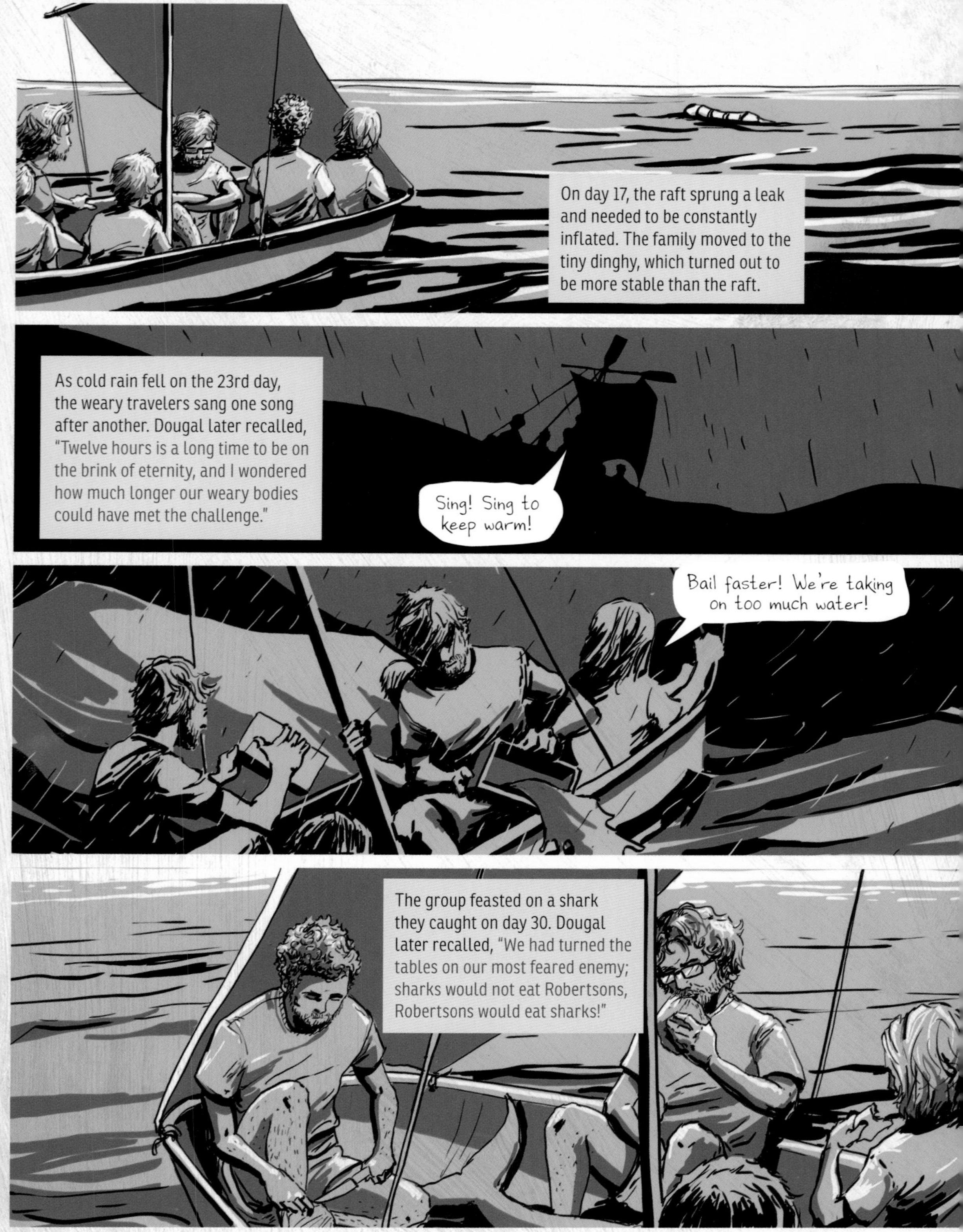
On day 17, the raft sprung a leak and needed to be constantly inflated. The family moved to the tiny dinghy, which turned out to be more stable than the raft.
As cold rain fell on the 23rd day, the weary travelers sang one song after another. Dougal later recalled, "Twelve hours is a long time to be on the brink of eternity, and I wondered how much longer our weary bodies could have met the challenge."
Sing! Sing to keep warm!
Bail faster! We're taking on too much water!
The group feasted on a shark they caught on day 30. Dougal later recalled, "We had turned the tables on our most feared enemy; sharks would not eat Robertsons, Robertsons would eat sharks!"

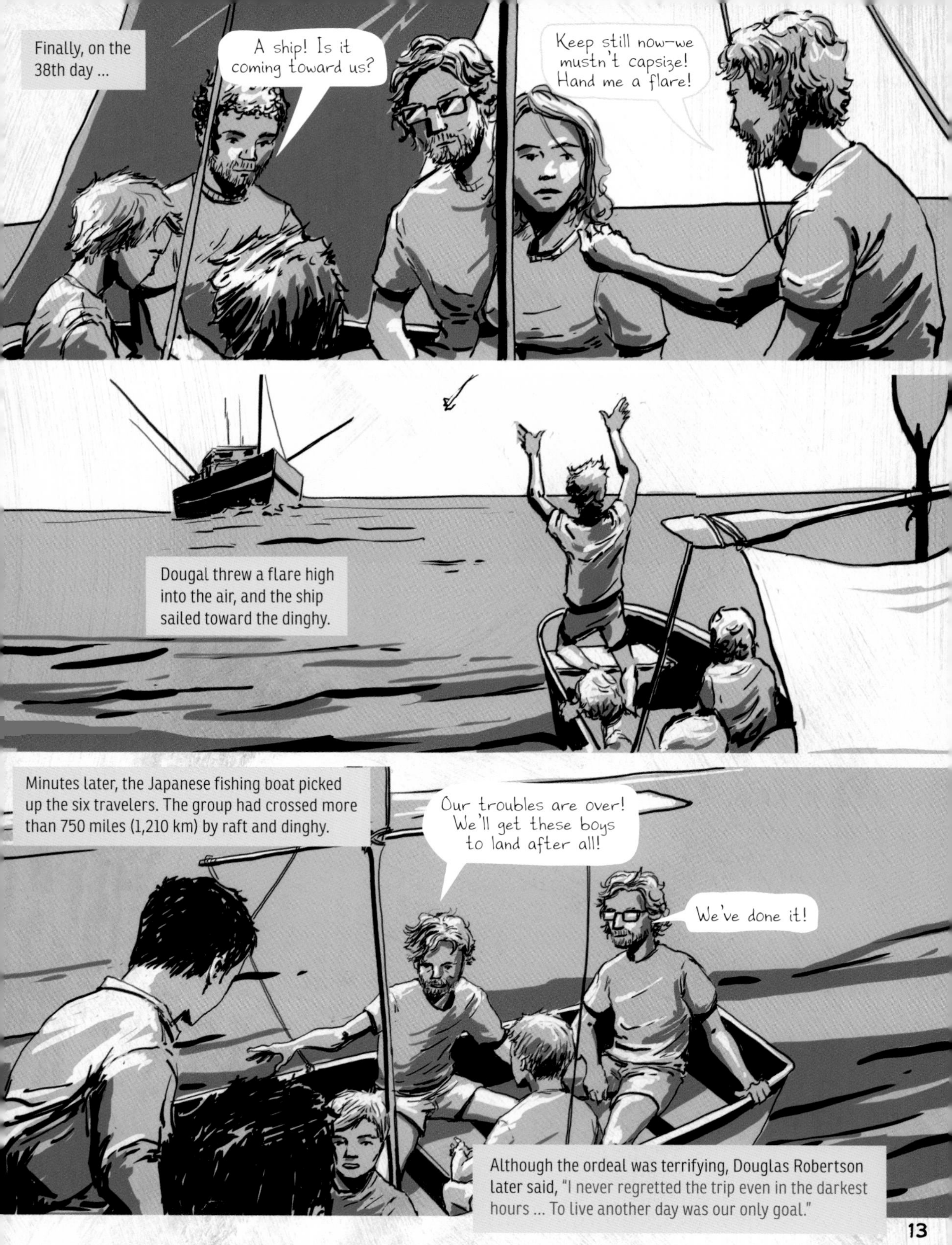
Finally, on the 38th day ...
A ship! Is it coming toward us?
Keep still now—we mustn't capsize! Hand me a flare!
Dougal threw a flare high into the air, and the ship sailed toward the dinghy.
Minutes later, the Japanese fishing boat picked up the six travelers. The group had crossed more than 750 miles (1,210 km) by raft and dinghy.
Our troubles are over! We'll get these boys to land after all!
We've done it!
Although the ordeal was terrifying, Douglas Robertson later said, "I never regretted the trip even in the darkest hours ... To live another day was our only goal."

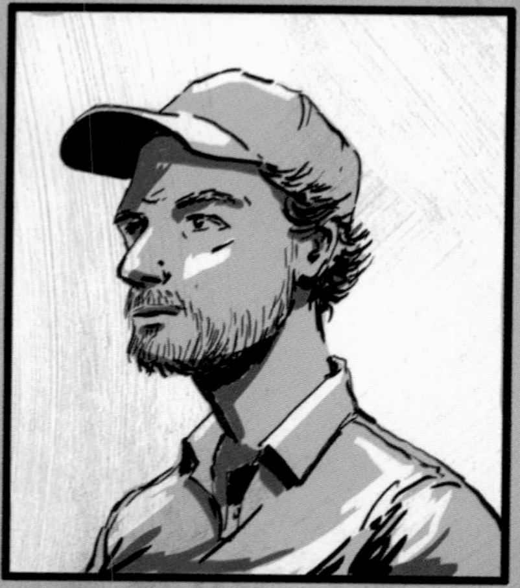

CHAPTER THREE

STEVEN CALLAHAN
ADRIFT AT SEA FOR 76 DAYS

On January 29, 1982, Steven Callahan set out from the Canary Islands. Sailing his 21-foot (6.4-meter) sloop, *Napoleon Solo*, Callahan was headed for the island of Antigua in the Caribbean Sea. The 29-year-old boat racer estimated he would arrive before February 25.

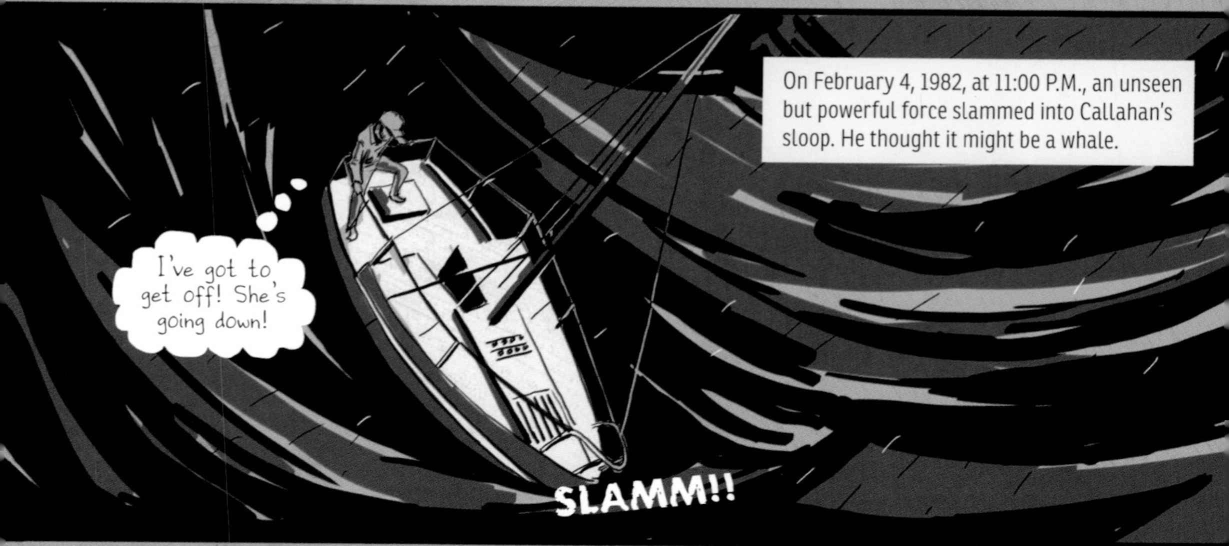
On February 4, 1982, at 11:00 P.M., an unseen but powerful force slammed into Callahan's sloop. He thought it might be a whale.
I've got to get off! She's going down!
SLAMM!!

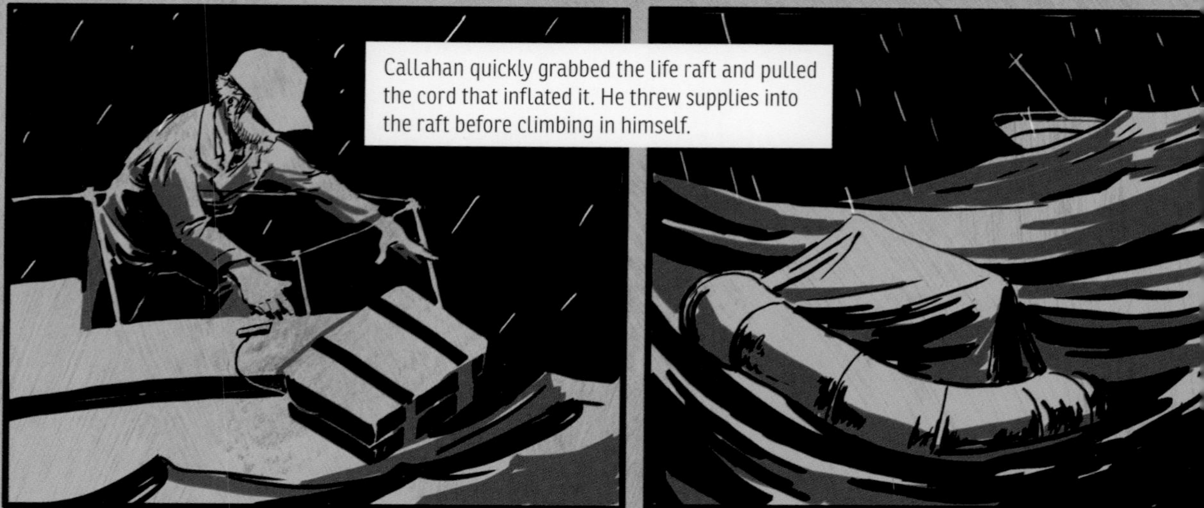
Callahan quickly grabbed the life raft and pulled the cord that inflated it. He threw supplies into the raft before climbing in himself.

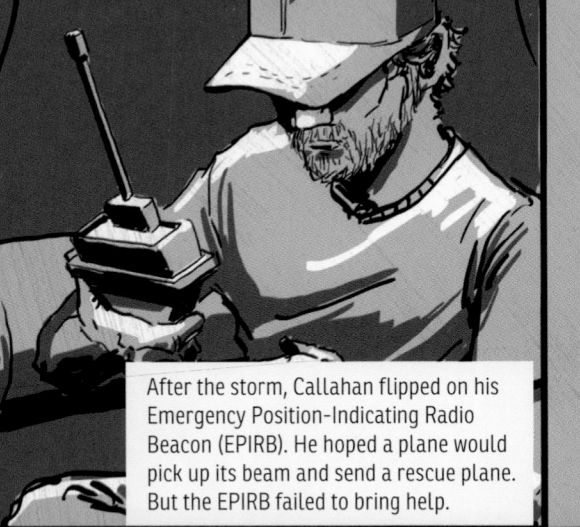

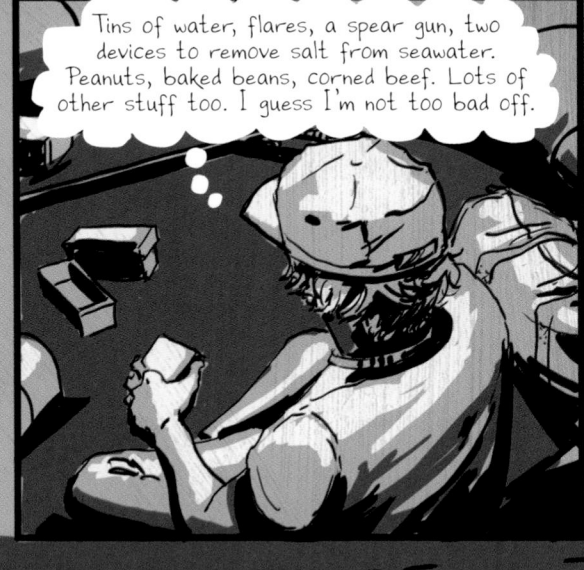

Tins of water, flares, a spear gun, two devices to remove salt from seawater. Peanuts, baked beans, corned beef. Lots of other stuff too. I guess I'm not too bad off.

After the storm, Callahan flipped on his Emergency Position-Indicating Radio Beacon (EPIRB). He hoped a plane would pick up its beam and send a rescue plane. But the EPIRB failed to bring help.

After 11 days, Callahan's tiny craft continued to float westward. He battled hunger, thirst, and the dangerous creatures of the ocean.

Keep away!

SWAK!

Day 13. Callahan knew he had to catch fish to survive. Finally, after several failed attempts ...

Got one!

Callahan caught many more fish. Soon he had 15 pounds (6.8 kilograms) of raw fish drying on clotheslines.

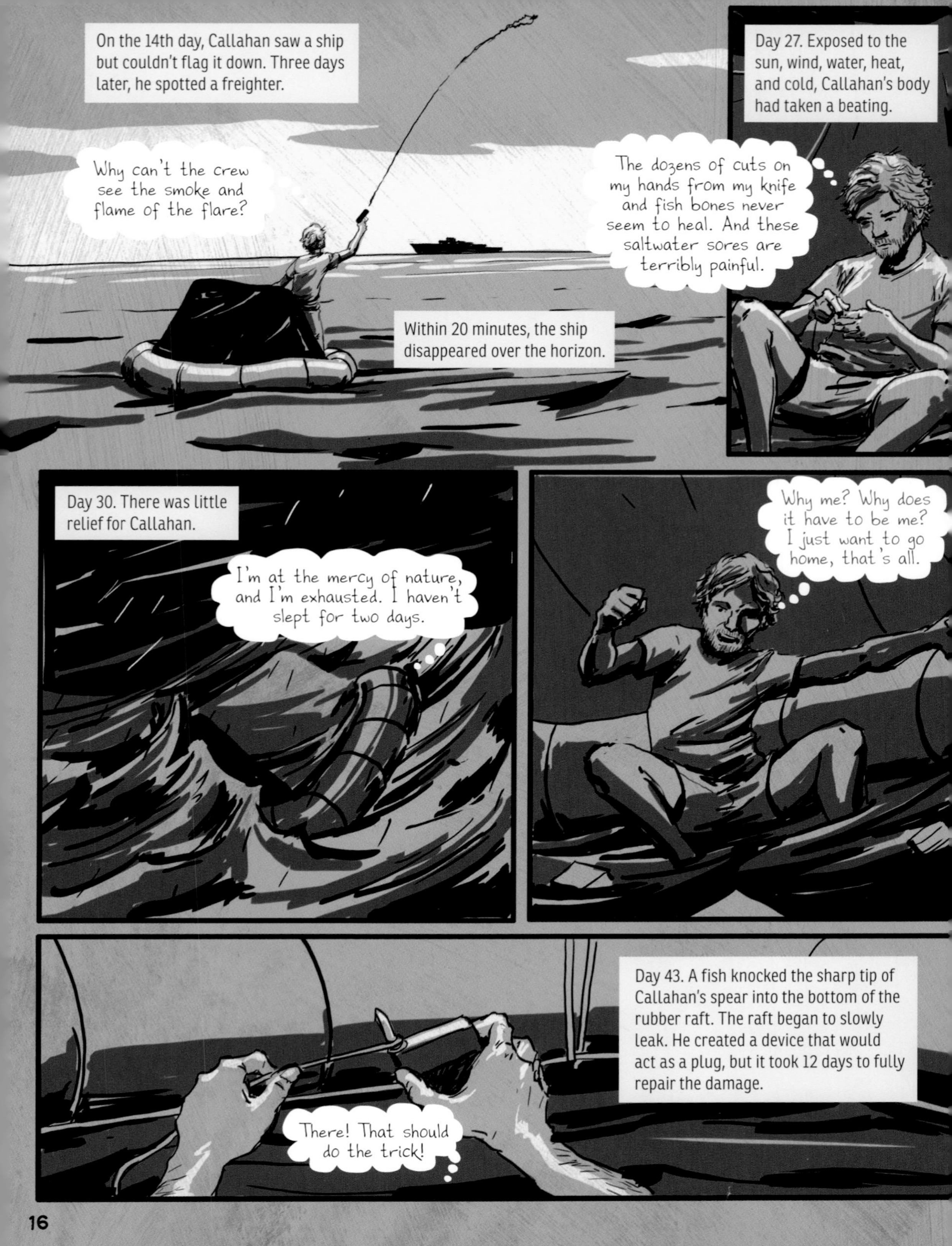

On the 14th day, Callahan saw a ship but couldn't flag it down. Three days later, he spotted a freighter.
Why can't the crew see the smoke and flame of the flare?
Within 20 minutes, the ship disappeared over the horizon.
Day 27. Exposed to the sun, wind, water, heat, and cold, Callahan's body had taken a beating.
The dozens of cuts on my hands from my knife and fish bones never seem to heal. And these saltwater sores are terribly painful.
Day 30. There was little relief for Callahan.
I'm at the mercy of nature, and I'm exhausted. I haven't slept for two days.
Why me? Why does it have to be me? I just want to go home, that's all.
Day 43. A fish knocked the sharp tip of Callahan's spear into the bottom of the rubber raft. The raft began to slowly leak. He created a device that would act as a plug, but it took 12 days to fully repair the damage.
There! That should do the trick!

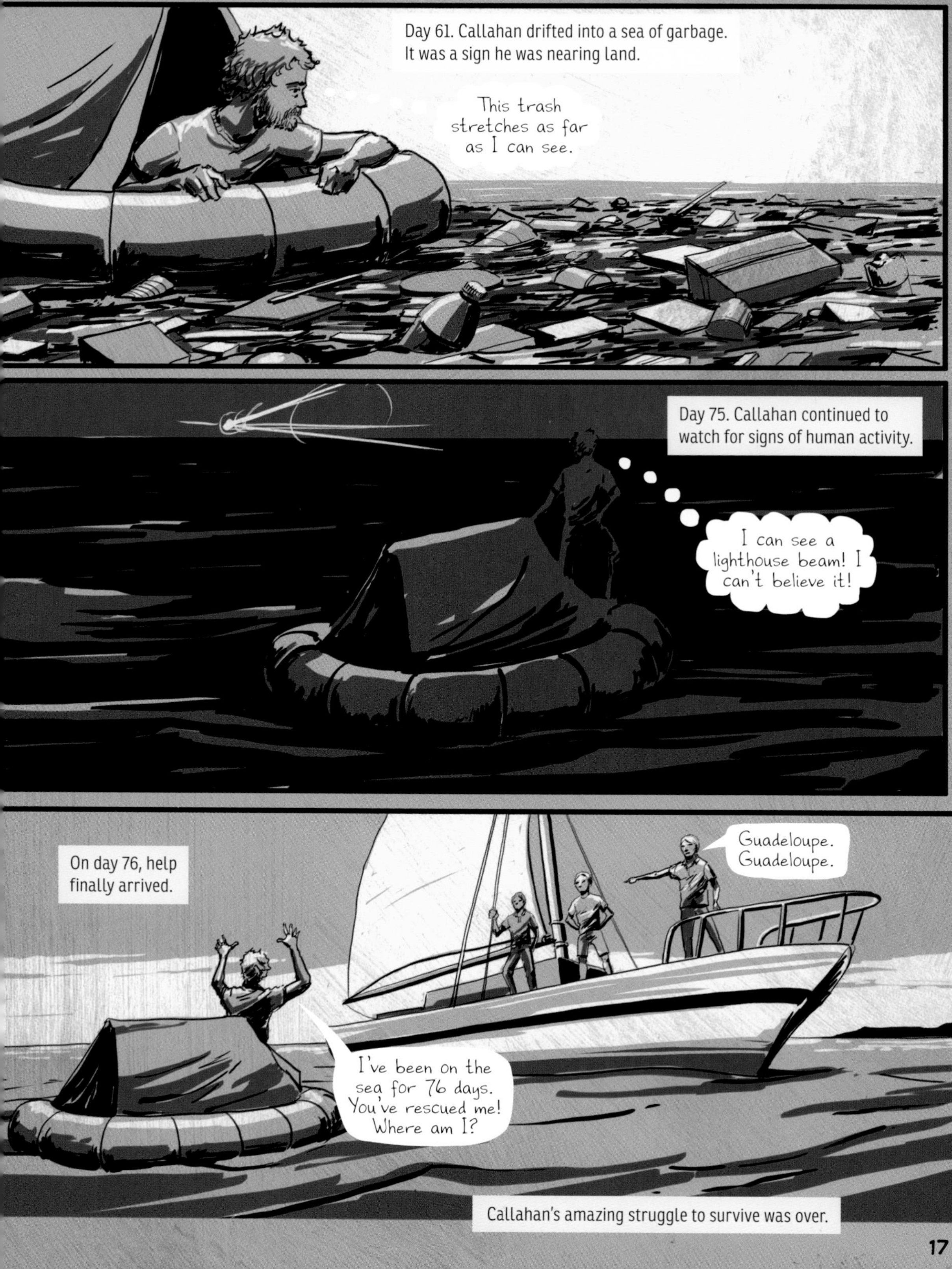
Day 61. Callahan drifted into a sea of garbage. It was a sign he was nearing land.
This trash stretches as far as I can see.
Day 75. Callahan continued to watch for signs of human activity.
I can see a lighthouse beam! I can't believe it!
On day 76, help finally arrived.
Guadeloupe. Guadeloupe.
I've been on the sea for 76 days. You've rescued me! Where am I?
Callahan's amazing struggle to survive was over.

CHAPTER FOUR

BOB KIDD

DEADLY DISASTER IN THE GULF OF ALASKA

Thirty-one-year-old Bob Kidd was a deck boss serving on the fishing vessel *St. Patrick* in the Gulf of Alaska. The crew fished the cold waters in search of scallops. On the night of November 29, 1981, a powerful storm packing 90-mile- (145-km-) per-hour winds roared into the gulf. The 12 crewmen aboard the 155-foot (47-m) ship faced near-certain doom. In fact, Kidd was one of only two men who survived the disaster.

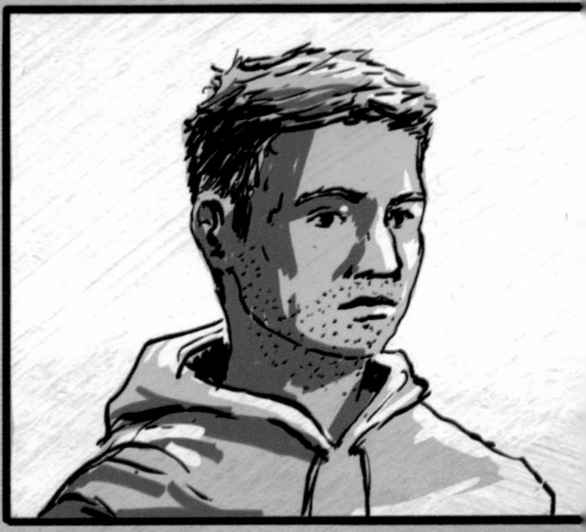

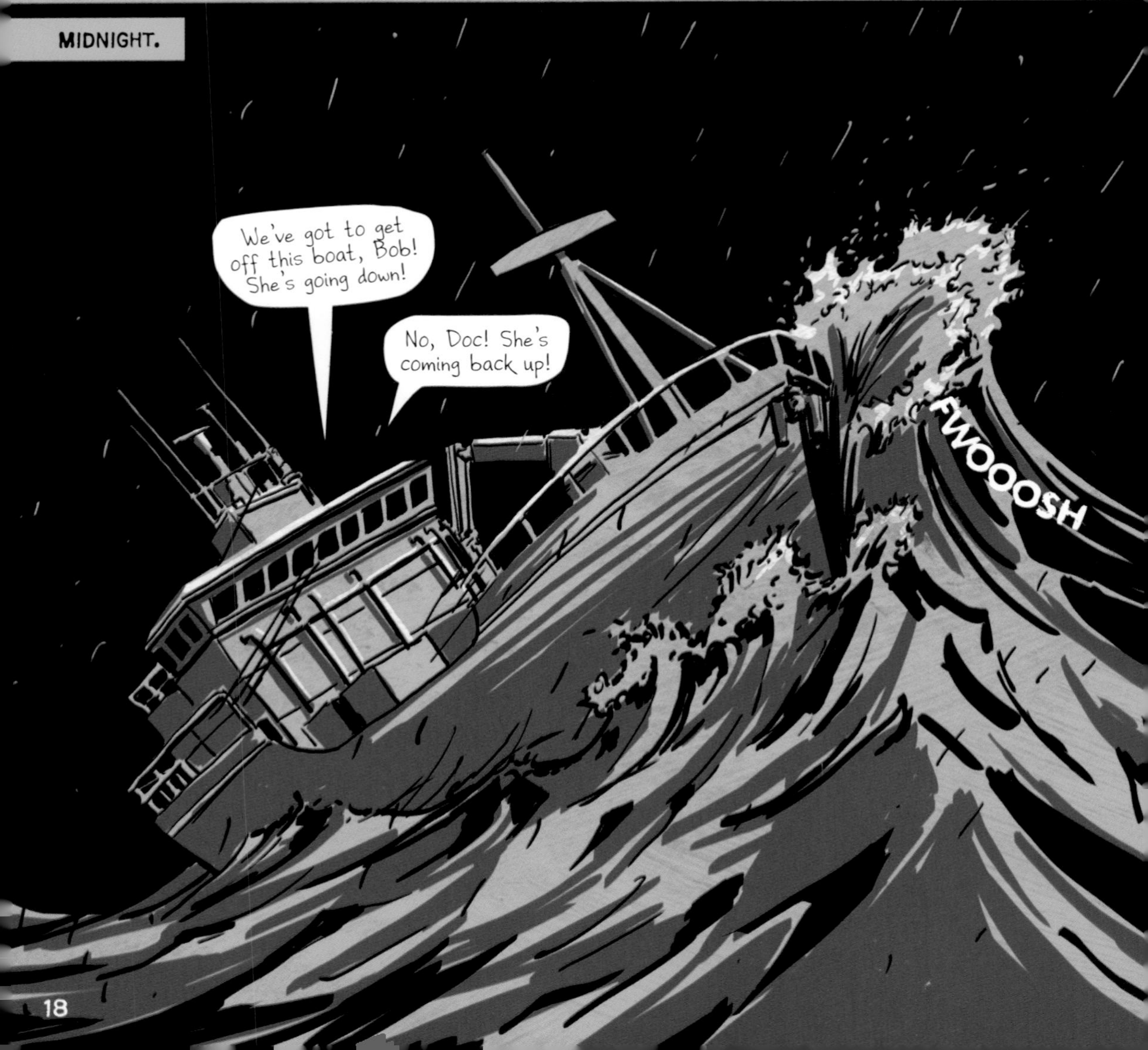
MIDNIGHT.
We've got to get off this boat, Bob! She's going down!
No, Doc! She's coming back up!
FWOOOOSH

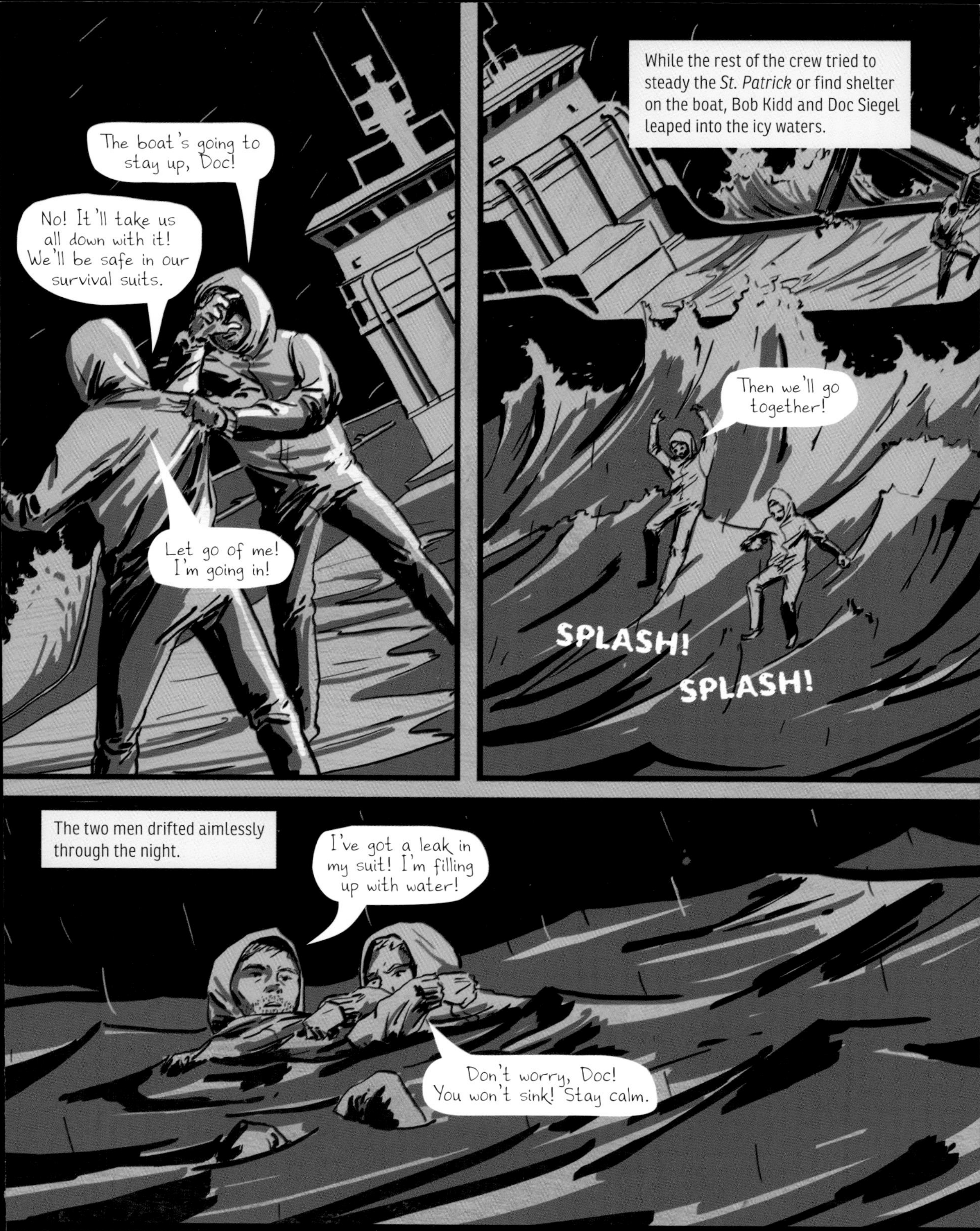
The boat's going to stay up, Doc!
No! It'll take us all down with it! We'll be safe in our survival suits.
Let go of me! I'm going in!
While the rest of the crew tried to steady the *St. Patrick* or find shelter on the boat, Bob Kidd and Doc Siegel leaped into the icy waters.
Then we'll go together!
SPLASH!
SPLASH!
The two men drifted aimlessly through the night.
I've got a leak in my suit! I'm filling up with water!
Don't worry, Doc! You won't sink! Stay calm.

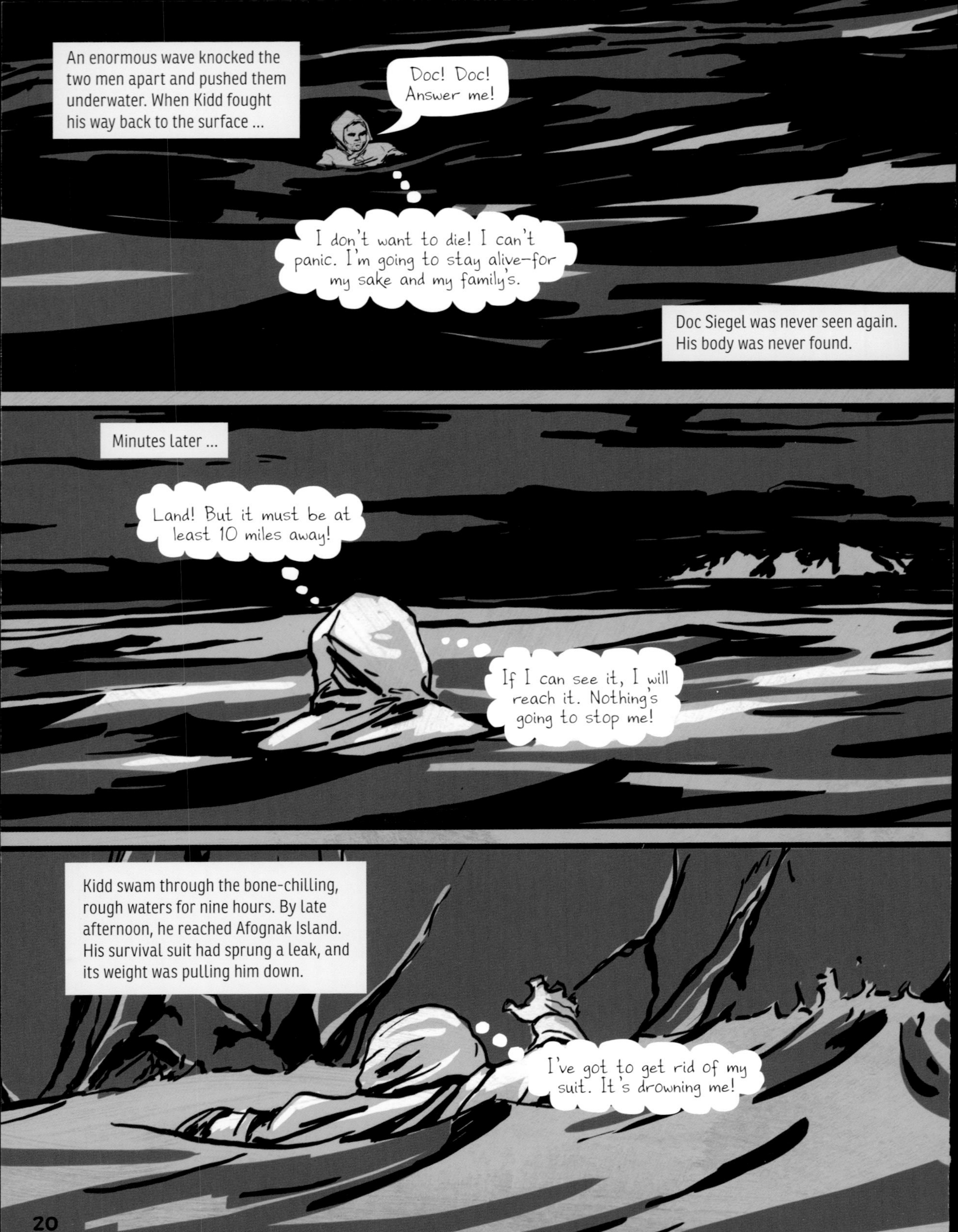
An enormous wave knocked the two men apart and pushed them underwater. When Kidd fought his way back to the surface ...
Doc! Doc! Answer me!
I don't want to die! I can't panic. I'm going to stay alive—for my sake and my family's.
Doc Siegel was never seen again. His body was never found.
Minutes later ...
Land! But it must be at least 10 miles away!
If I can see it, I will reach it. Nothing's going to stop me!
Kidd swam through the bone-chilling, rough waters for nine hours. By late afternoon, he reached Afognak Island. His survival suit had sprung a leak, and its weight was pulling him down.
I've got to get rid of my suit. It's drowning me!

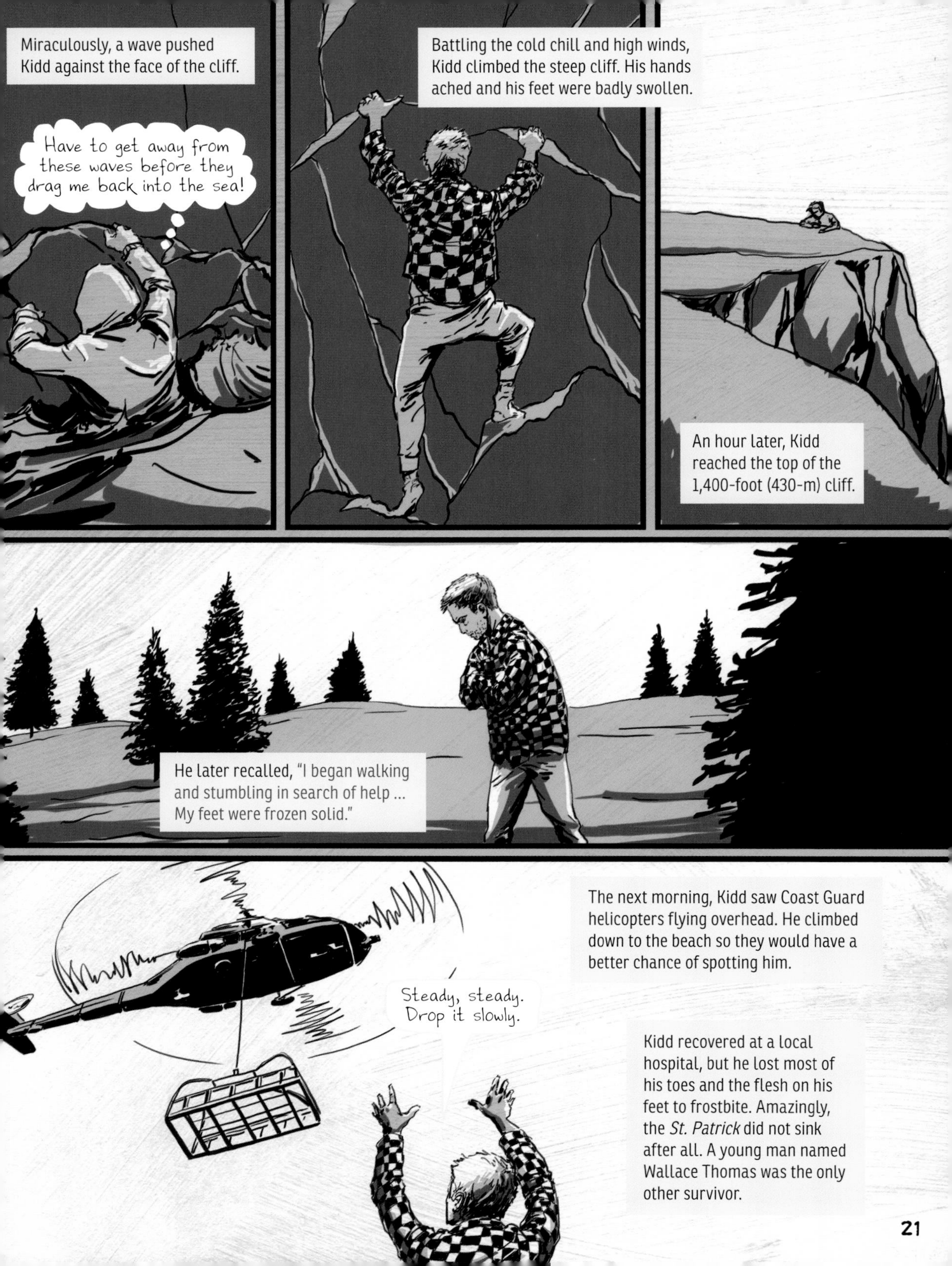
Miraculously, a wave pushed Kidd against the face of the cliff.
Have to get away from these waves before they drag me back into the sea!
Battling the cold chill and high winds, Kidd climbed the steep cliff. His hands ached and his feet were badly swollen.
An hour later, Kidd reached the top of the 1,400-foot (430-m) cliff.
He later recalled, "I began walking and stumbling in search of help ... My feet were frozen solid."
The next morning, Kidd saw Coast Guard helicopters flying overhead. He climbed down to the beach so they would have a better chance of spotting him.
Steady, steady. Drop it slowly.
Kidd recovered at a local hospital, but he lost most of his toes and the flesh on his feet to frostbite. Amazingly, the *St. Patrick* did not sink after all. A young man named Wallace Thomas was the only other survivor.

CHAPTER FIVE

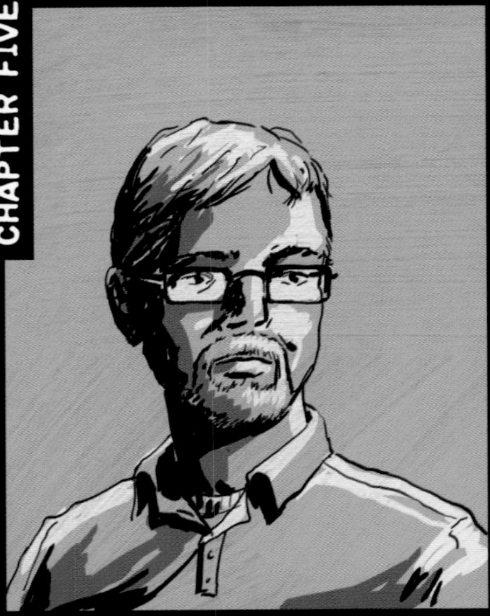

RICHARD PHILLIPS

CAPTURED BY SOMALI PIRATES

Richard Phillips served as the captain of the *Maersk Alabama* container ship in April 2009. The ship was traveling from Oman to Kenya with a crew of about 20. It carried thousands of tons of cargo, including relief supplies for Kenya, Somalia, and Uganda. Phillips and his crew were warned by U.S. authorities that Somali pirates were in the area. For days, the *Alabama* dodged a skiff of pirates, but in the end, the ship was too large to outrun the swift craft. That's when the pirates attacked.

APRIL 8, 2009. 280 MILES (450 KM) OFF THE COAST OF SOMALIA.

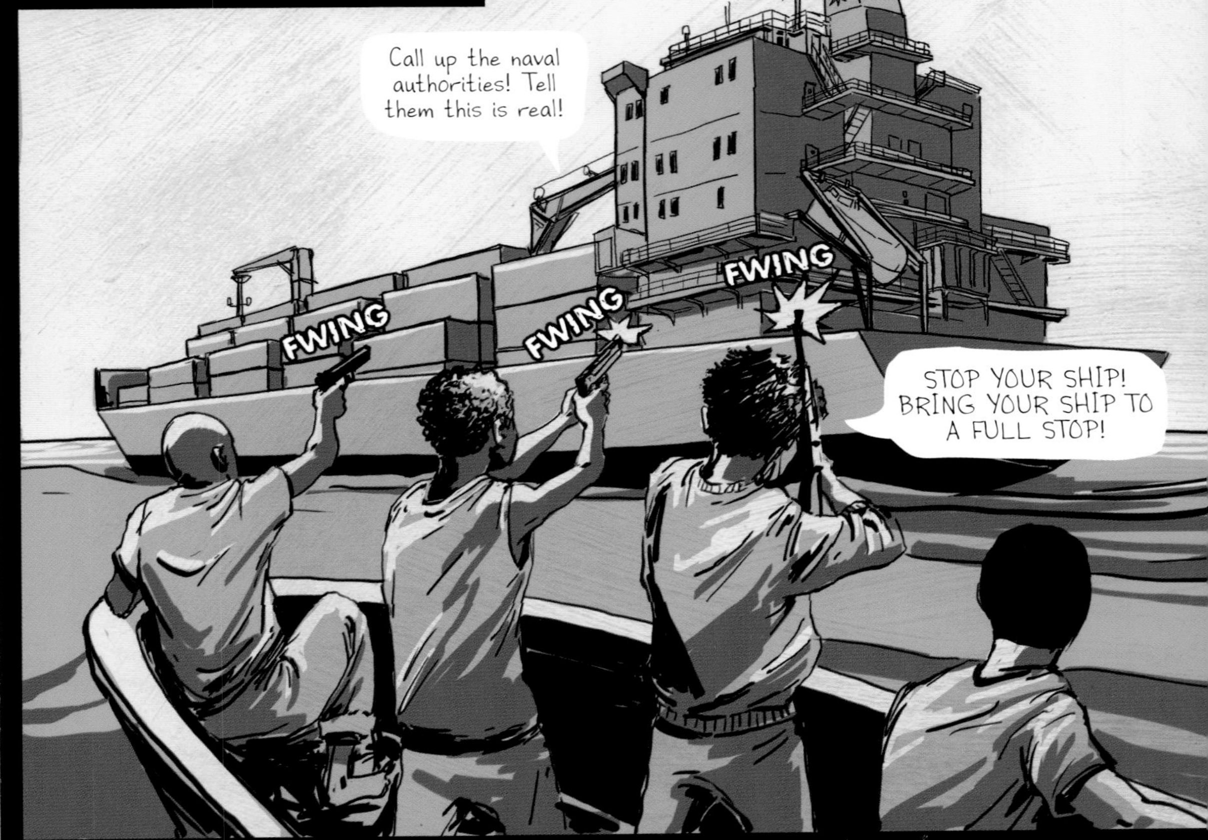
Call up the naval authorities! Tell them this is real!
FWING
FWING
FWING
STOP YOUR SHIP! BRING YOUR SHIP TO A FULL STOP!

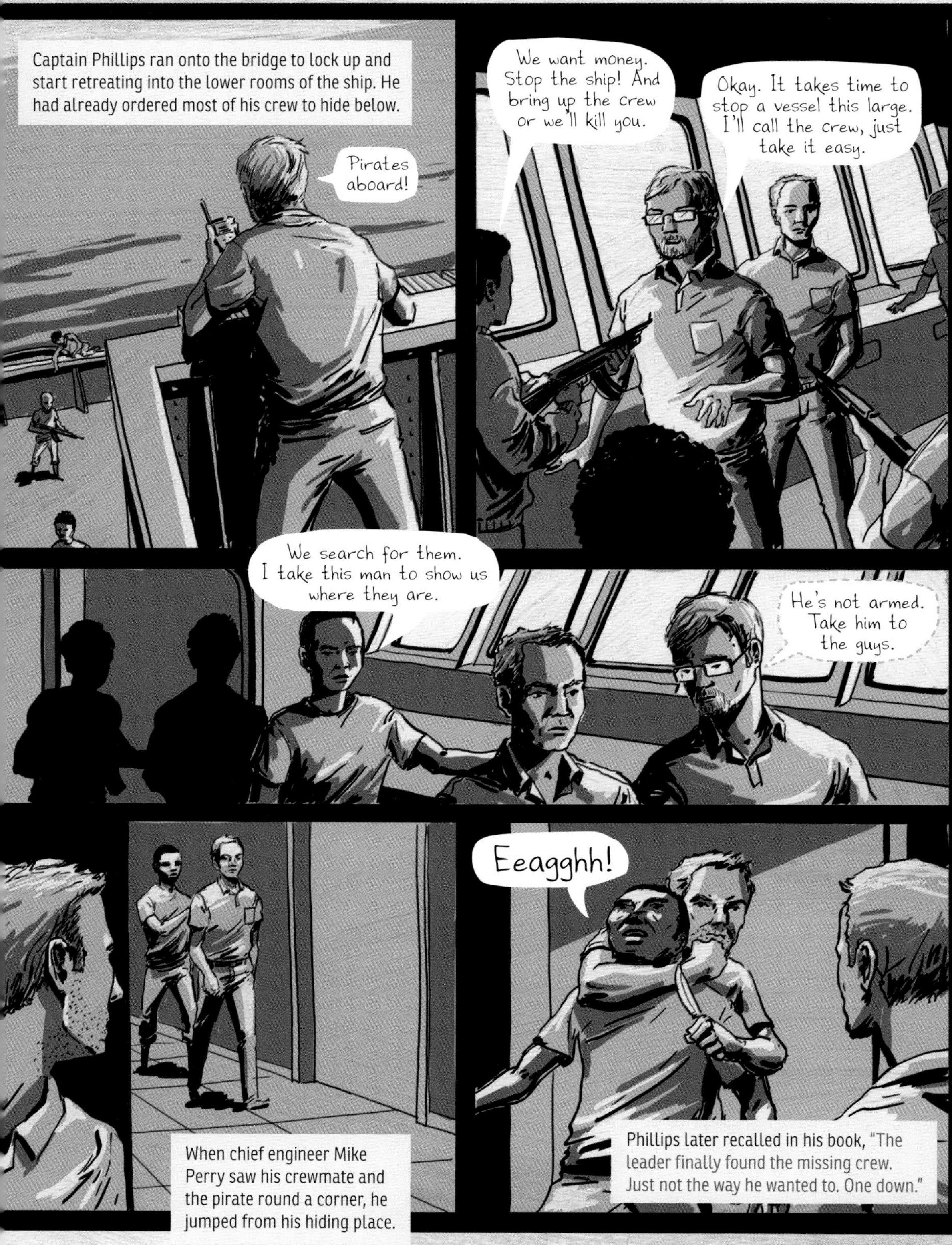
Captain Phillips ran onto the bridge to lock up and start retreating into the lower rooms of the ship. He had already ordered most of his crew to hide below.
Pirates aboard!
We want money. Stop the ship! And bring up the crew or we'll kill you.
Okay. It takes time to stop a vessel this large. I'll call the crew, just take it easy.
We search for them. I take this man to show us where they are.
He's not armed. Take him to the guys.
When chief engineer Mike Perry saw his crewmate and the pirate round a corner, he jumped from his hiding place.
Eeagghh!
Phillips later recalled in his book, "The leader finally found the missing crew. Just not the way he wanted to. One down."

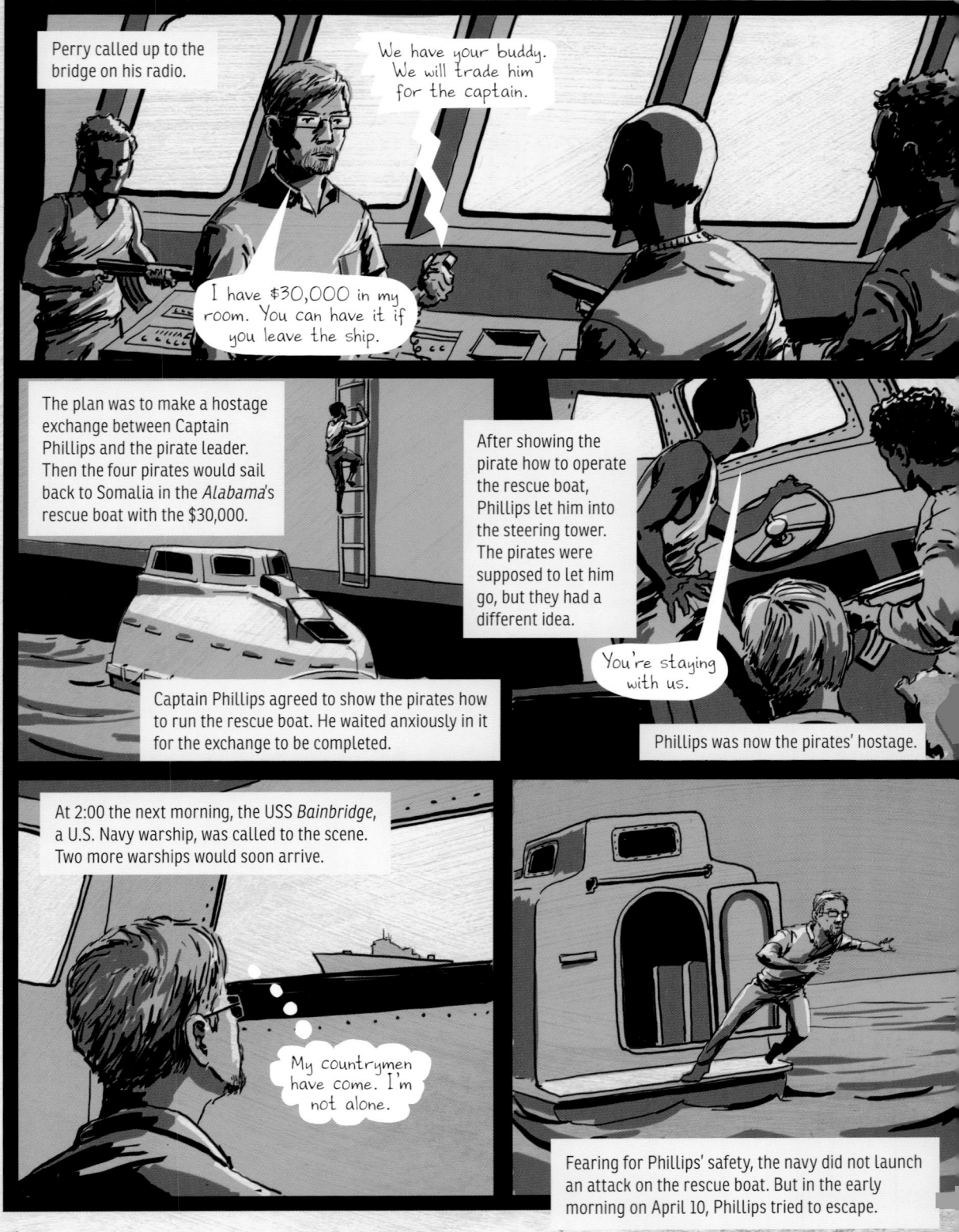

Perry called up to the bridge on his radio.

We have your buddy. We will trade him for the captain.

I have $30,000 in my room. You can have it if you leave the ship.

The plan was to make a hostage exchange between Captain Phillips and the pirate leader. Then the four pirates would sail back to Somalia in the *Alabama*'s rescue boat with the $30,000.

After showing the pirate how to operate the rescue boat, Phillips let him into the steering tower. The pirates were supposed to let him go, but they had a different idea.

Captain Phillips agreed to show the pirates how to run the rescue boat. He waited anxiously in it for the exchange to be completed.

You're staying with us.

Phillips was now the pirates' hostage.

At 2:00 the next morning, the USS *Bainbridge*, a U.S. Navy warship, was called to the scene. Two more warships would soon arrive.

My countrymen have come. I'm not alone.

Fearing for Phillips' safety, the navy did not launch an attack on the rescue boat. But in the early morning on April 10, Phillips tried to escape.

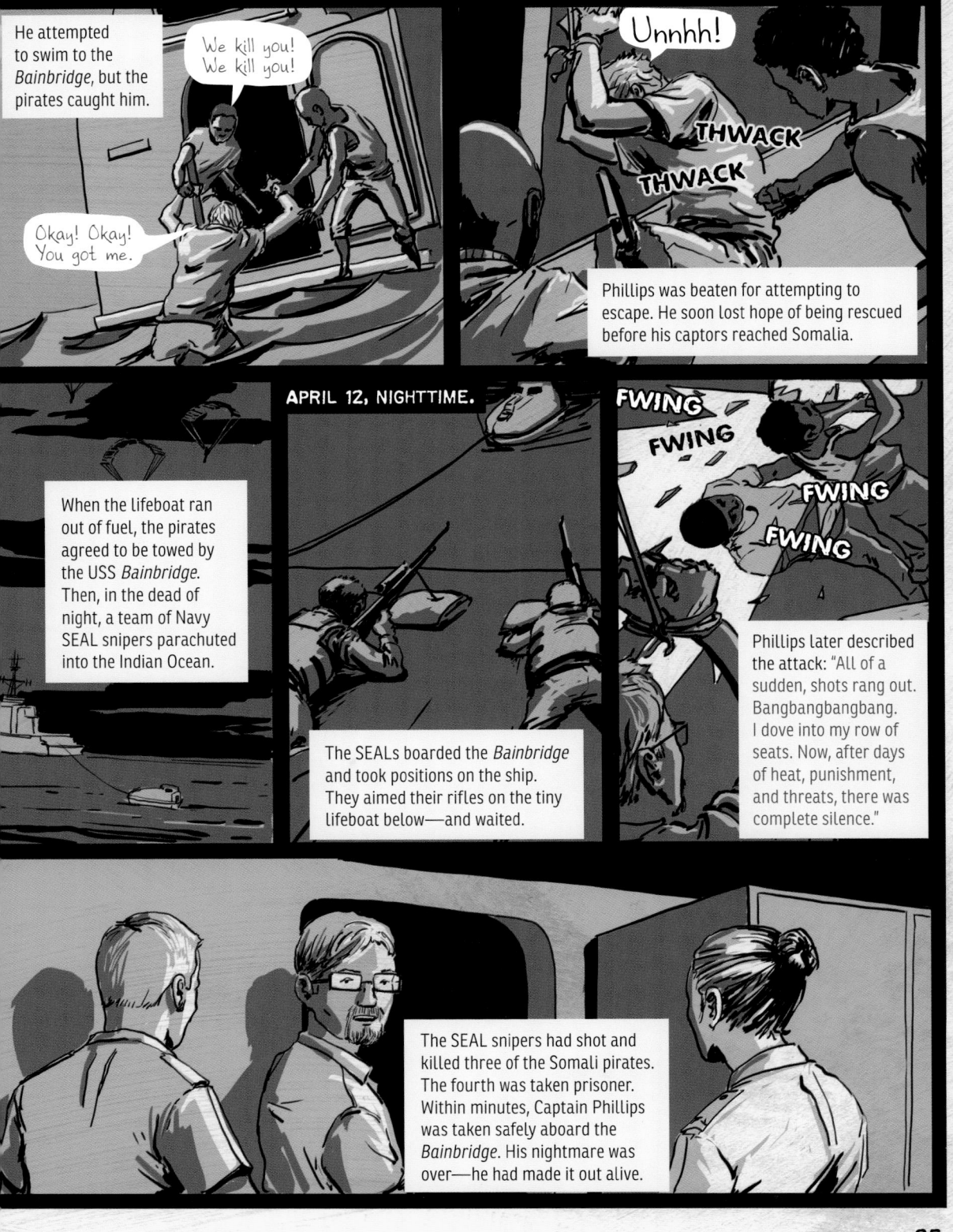

He attempted to swim to the *Bainbridge*, but the pirates caught him.

We kill you! We kill you!

Okay! Okay! You got me.

Unnhh!

THWACK

THWACK

Phillips was beaten for attempting to escape. He soon lost hope of being rescued before his captors reached Somalia.

When the lifeboat ran out of fuel, the pirates agreed to be towed by the USS *Bainbridge*. Then, in the dead of night, a team of Navy SEAL snipers parachuted into the Indian Ocean.

APRIL 12, NIGHTTIME.

The SEALs boarded the *Bainbridge* and took positions on the ship. They aimed their rifles on the tiny lifeboat below—and waited.

FWING

FWING

FWING

FWING

Phillips later described the attack: "All of a sudden, shots rang out. Bangbangbangbang. I dove into my row of seats. Now, after days of heat, punishment, and threats, there was complete silence."

The SEAL snipers had shot and killed three of the Somali pirates. The fourth was taken prisoner. Within minutes, Captain Phillips was taken safely aboard the *Bainbridge*. His nightmare was over—he had made it out alive.

CHAPTER SIX

HIROMITSU SHINKAWA

VICTIM OF A DEADLY TSUNAMI

On March 11, 2011, a tsunami slammed into Minamisoma on the northeastern coast of Japan. Sixty-year-old Hiromitsu Shinkawa was on the second floor of his home when the powerful wave struck. The tsunami tore apart the house and swept Shinkawa into the rushing waters.

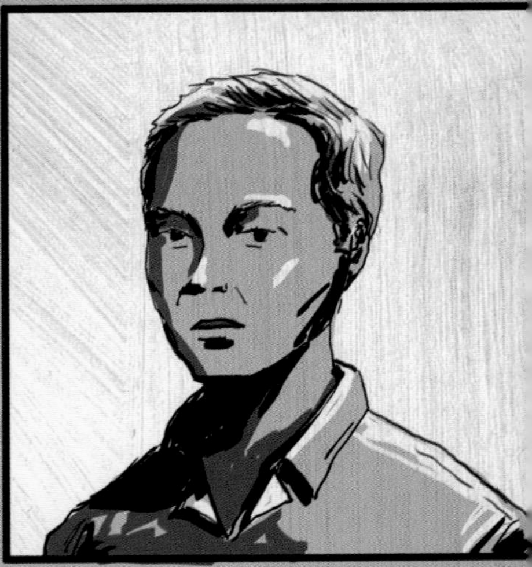

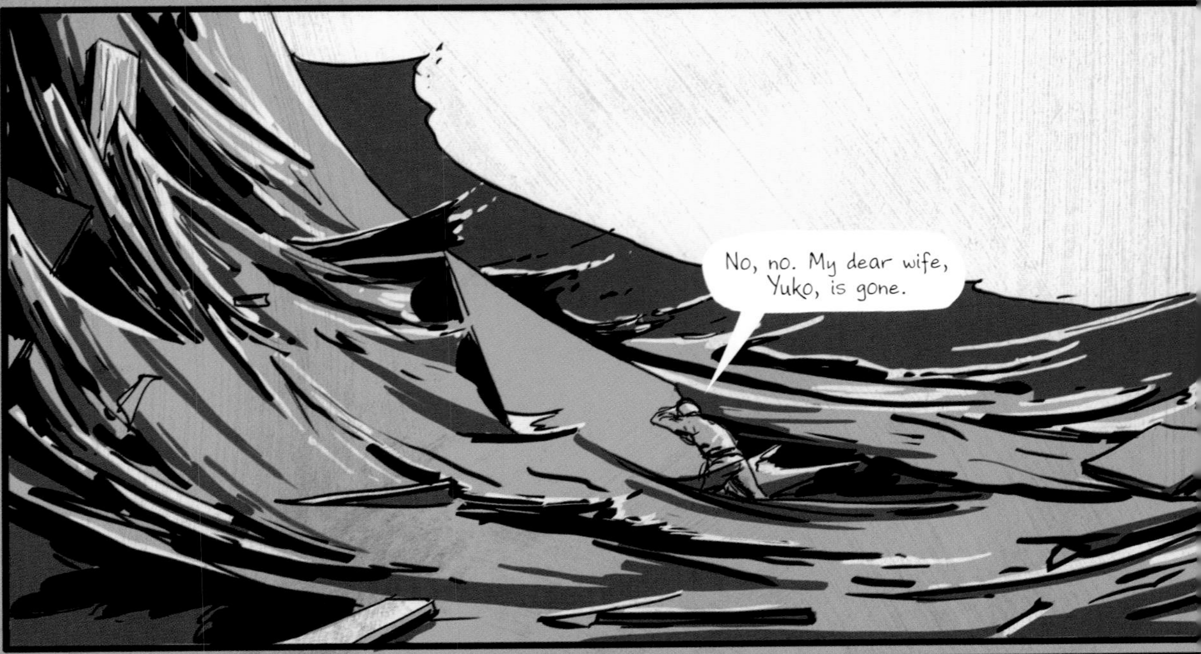
No, no. My dear wife, Yuko, is gone.

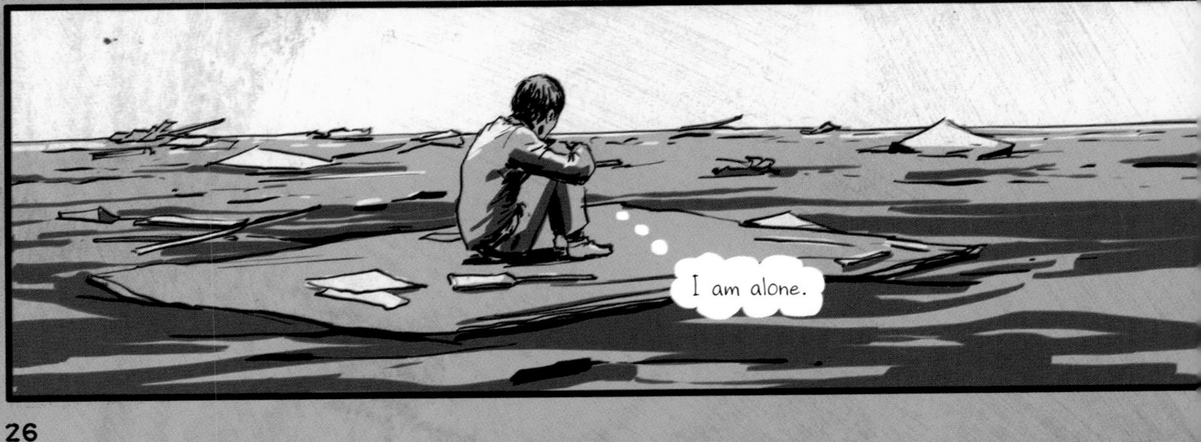
I am alone.

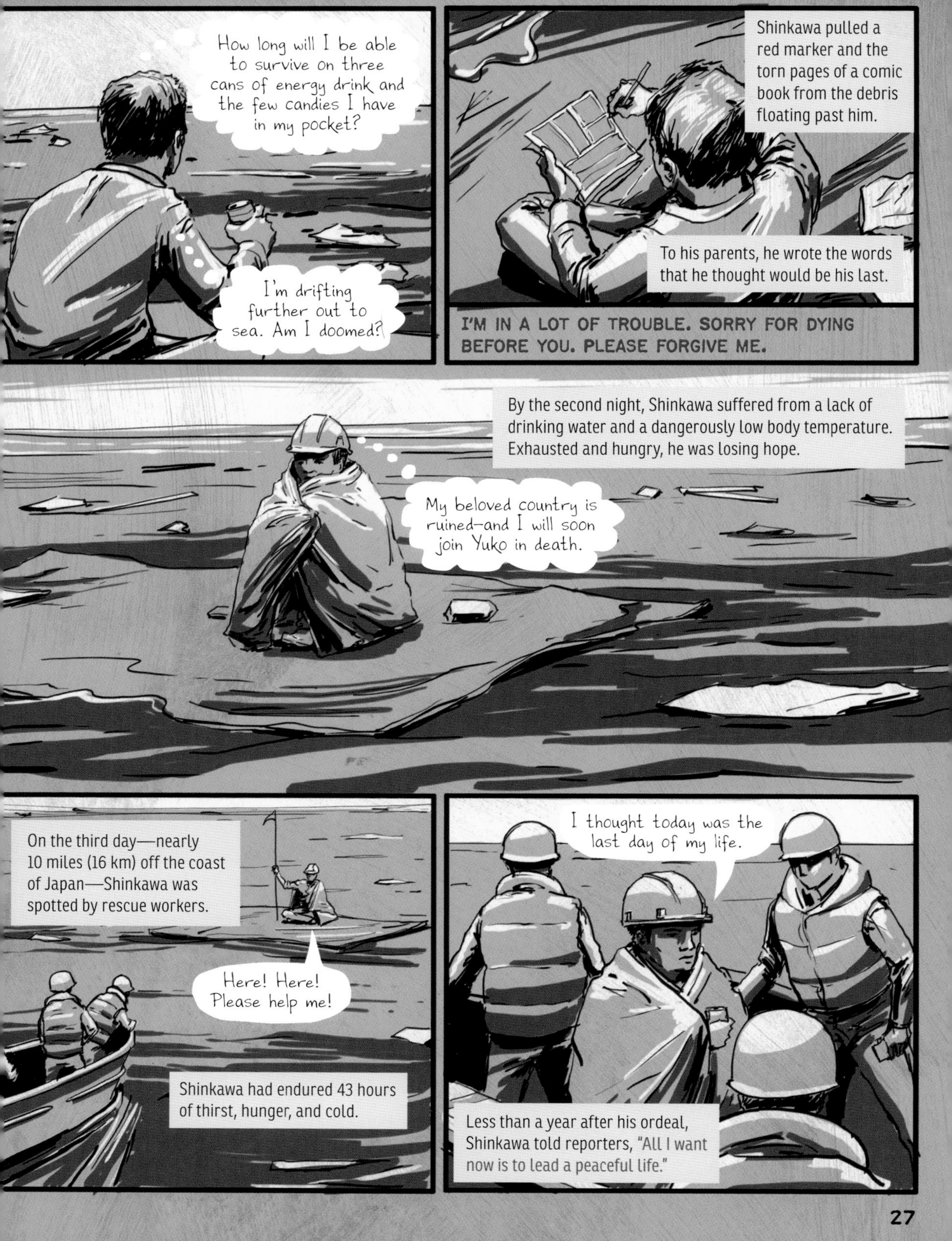
How long will I be able to survive on three cans of energy drink and the few candies I have in my pocket?
I'm drifting further out to sea. Am I doomed?
Shinkawa pulled a red marker and the torn pages of a comic book from the debris floating past him.
To his parents, he wrote the words that he thought would be his last.
I'M IN A LOT OF TROUBLE. SORRY FOR DYING BEFORE YOU. PLEASE FORGIVE ME.
By the second night, Shinkawa suffered from a lack of drinking water and a dangerously low body temperature. Exhausted and hungry, he was losing hope.
My beloved country is ruined—and I will soon join Yuko in death.
On the third day—nearly 10 miles (16 km) off the coast of Japan—Shinkawa was spotted by rescue workers.
Here! Here! Please help me!
Shinkawa had endured 43 hours of thirst, hunger, and cold.
I thought today was the last day of my life.
Less than a year after his ordeal, Shinkawa told reporters, "All I want now is to lead a peaceful life."

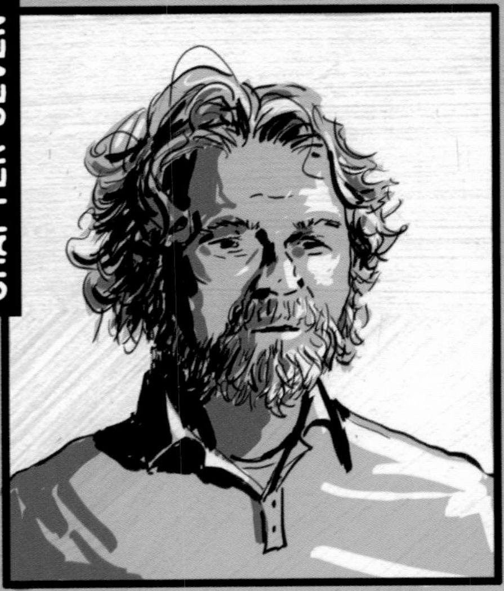

CHAPTER SEVEN

JOSE SALVADOR ALVARENGA
FACT OR FICTION?

On December 21, 2012, 36-year-old Jose Salvador Alvarenga and 23-year-old Ezekiel Cordova set out on a fishing trip from southern Mexico. On their first day at sea, a storm blew their 26-foot (7.9-m) motorboat off course and damaged its engines. The two men drifted across the Pacific Ocean.

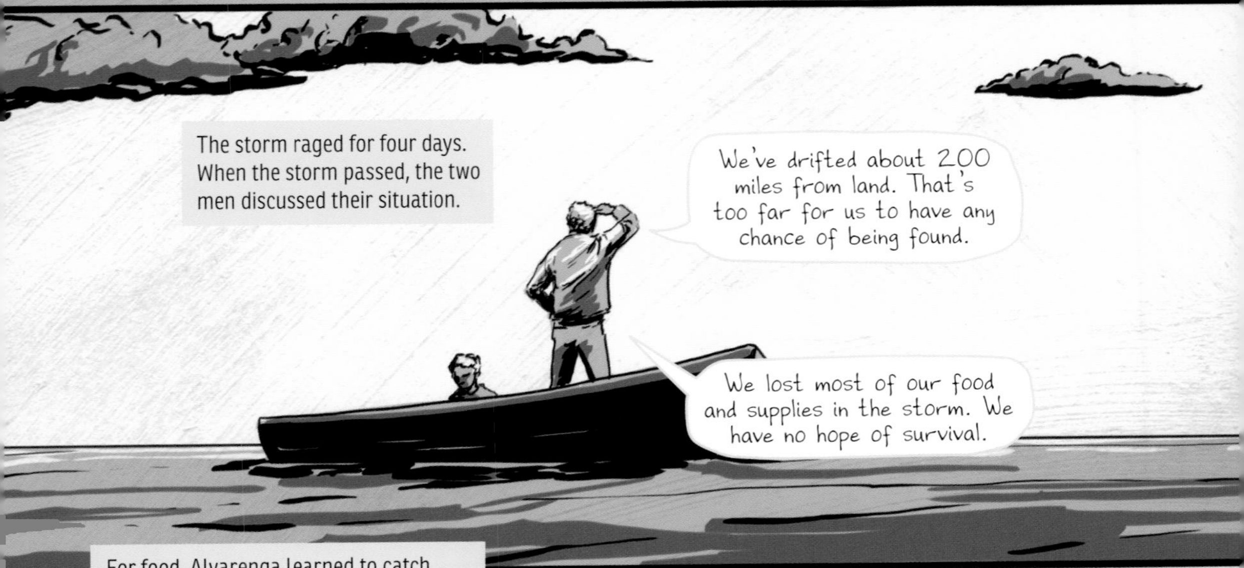
The storm raged for four days. When the storm passed, the two men discussed their situation.
We've drifted about 200 miles from land. That's too far for us to have any chance of being found.
We lost most of our food and supplies in the storm. We have no hope of survival.

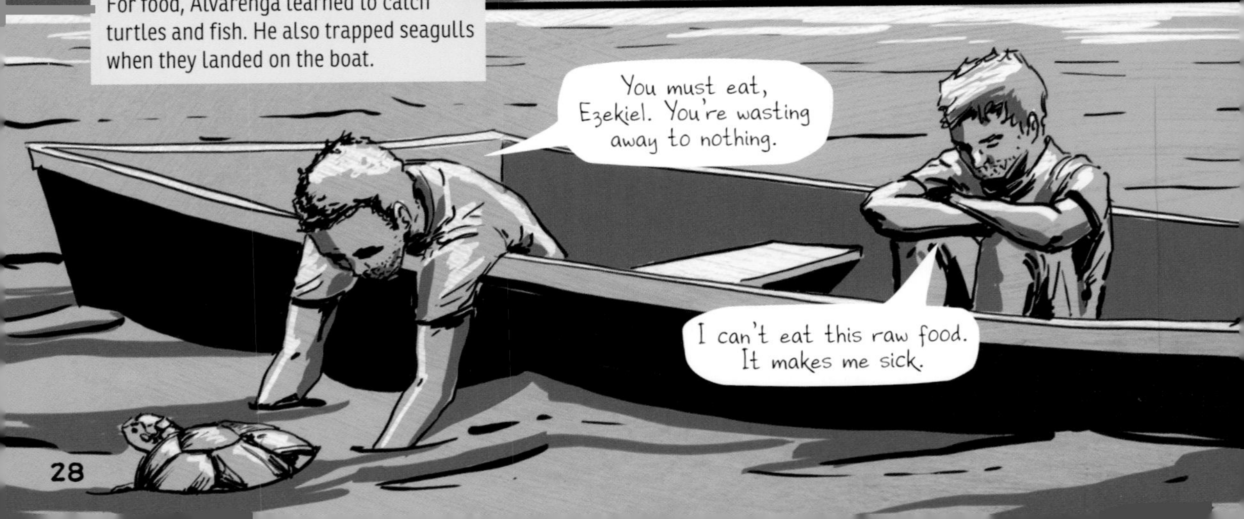
For food, Alvarenga learned to catch turtles and fish. He also trapped seagulls when they landed on the boat.
You must eat, Ezekiel. You're wasting away to nothing.
I can't eat this raw food. It makes me sick.

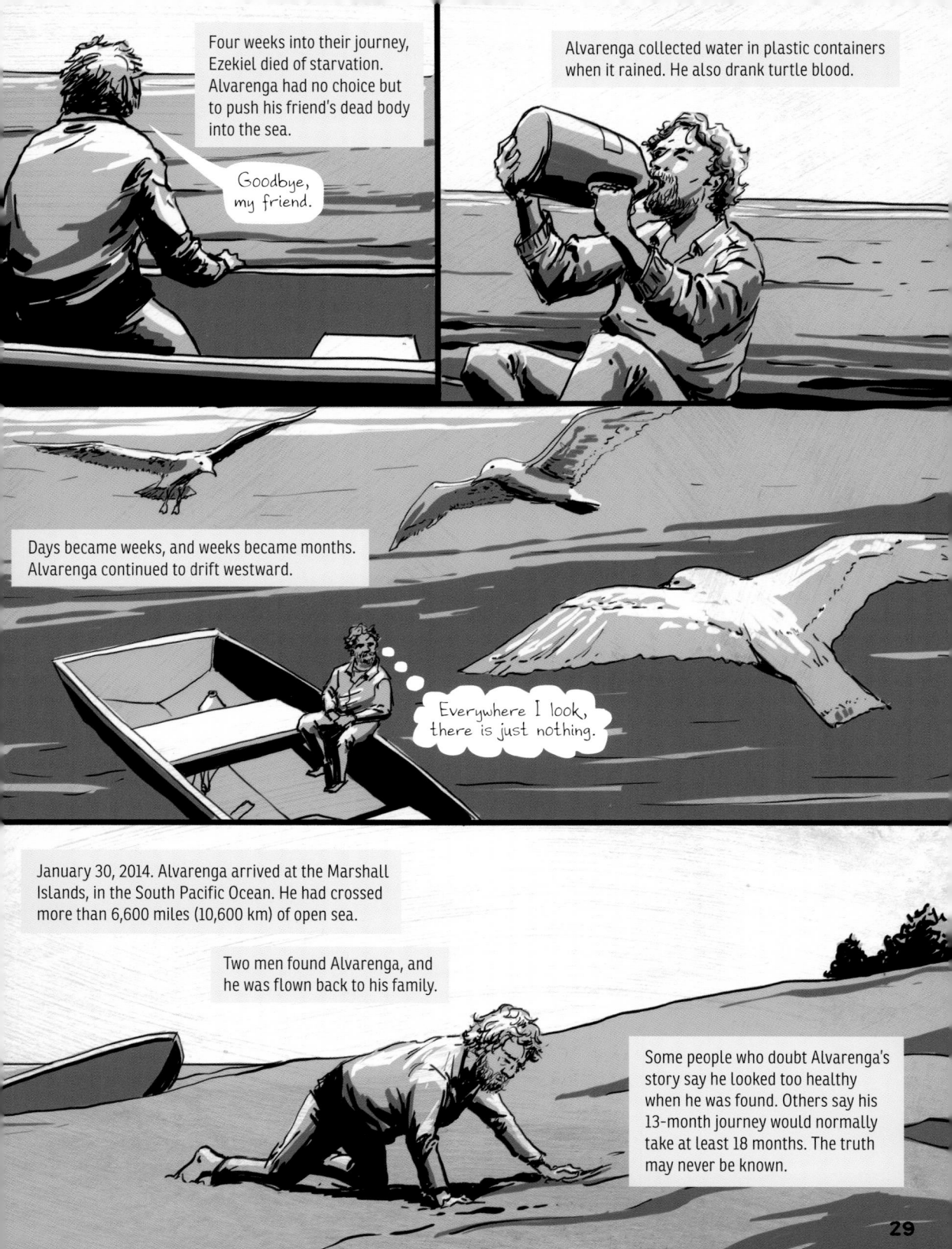

Four weeks into their journey, Ezekiel died of starvation. Alvarenga had no choice but to push his friend's dead body into the sea.

Goodbye, my friend.

Alvarenga collected water in plastic containers when it rained. He also drank turtle blood.

Days became weeks, and weeks became months. Alvarenga continued to drift westward.

Everywhere I look, there is just nothing.

January 30, 2014. Alvarenga arrived at the Marshall Islands, in the South Pacific Ocean. He had crossed more than 6,600 miles (10,600 km) of open sea.

Two men found Alvarenga, and he was flown back to his family.

Some people who doubt Alvarenga's story say he looked too healthy when he was found. Others say his 13-month journey would normally take at least 18 months. The truth may never be known.

GLOSSARY

BARNACLE *(BARR-ni-kuhl)*—a small shellfish that attaches itself to the sides of ships

BRIDGE *(BRIJ)*—the control center of a ship

CAPSIZE *(KAP-size)*—to tip over in the water

CARGO *(KAHR-goh)*—the goods carried by a ship, aircraft, or other vehicle

DINGHY *(DING-ee)*—a small boat

FLARE *(FLAIR)*—a burst of light shot from a gun to announce one's presence or position

INFLATE *(in-FLAYT)*—to make something expand by blowing or pumping air into it

SCALLOP *(SKAL-uhp)*—an edible shellfish that swims by snapping its shells together and shooting out a jet of water

SCHOONER *(SKOON-ur)*—a ship with masts at the front and back

SKIFF *(SKIF)*—a shallow, flat-bottomed boat

SLOOP *(SLOOP)*—a sailboat with one mast and sails that are set from front to back

SNIPER *(SNIE-pur)*—a soldier trained to shoot at long-distance targets from a hidden place

STEWARD *(STOO-urd)*—the ship's officer who is in charge of food and meals; a steward is also an attendant on a ship

READ MORE

Lassieur, Allison. *Can You Survive Being Lost at Sea?: An Interactive Survival Adventure.* North Mankato, Minn.: Capstone Press, 2013.

McNab, Chris. *Survival at Sea.* Broomall, Penn.: Mason Crest Publishers, 2014.

Mooney, Carla. *Surviving in Wild Waters.* Minneapolis, Minn.: Lerner Publications, 2014.

Yomtov, Nel. *Terrors from the Deep.* True Tales of Survival. North Mankato, Minn.: Capstone Press, 2015.

INTERNET SITES

FactHound offers a safe, fun way to find Internet sites related to this book. All of the sites on FactHound have been researched by our staff.

Here's all you do:

Visit *www.facthound.com*

Type in this code: 9781491465721

Super-cool stuff!

Check out projects, games and lots more at
www.capstonekids.com

INDEX